Murder Squad

MURDER SQUAD

Tim Tate and Ray Wyre

Thames Methuen

First published in Great Britain 1992
by Methuen London
Michelin House, 81 Fulham Road, London SW3 6RB
in association with Thames Television International Ltd
149 Tottenham Court Road, London W1P 9LL

Copyright © 1992 by Tim Tate, Ray Wyre
and Thames Television plc

The authors have asserted their moral rights

A CIP catalogue record for this book
is available from the British Library
ISBN 0 413 64560 6

Typeset by Deltatype Ltd, Ellesmere Port

Printed in Great Britain
by Clays Ltd, St Ives plc

Contents

List of Illustrations

Acknowledgements and thanks for permission to reproduce photographs are due as follows: Ordnance Survey (photograph by Nicky Johnston) for plate 1; Metropolitan Police for plates 2a, 2b, 3a, 3b, 4a, 5a and 5b; Argo Productions Ltd for plates 4b, 4c and 7a; Nicky Johnston for plates 6a, 6b and 7b; HMSO for plate 8.

Acknowledgements   We would like to
thank the men and women of the Metropolitan
Police Service for their assistance and patience
in taking us into their working lives. We also
owe a debt of thanks to those of the victims'
families who found the courage to talk about a
still painful event.

Finally, we would like to thank all the staff
at Gracewell Clinic for their help and advice.

Introduction

Why murder? What is it about the taking of a life which simultaneously so fascinates and revolts?

From Marple to Morse, Poirot to Wexford, the act and detection of homicide has attracted a loyal following amongst consumers of detective fiction. And with fiction, so fact. 'True Crime' books are amongst the most popular of all non-fiction published today. Inevitably murder – the gorier the better – is the most common theme.

When we were approached to write this book – itself a companion to a television documentary series aimed squarely at a popular audience – we both had, in different ways, some experience of the reality of murder.

As a probation officer and later a therapist, Ray had worked – and indeed still does – extensively with some of Britain's most notorious killers, from the gangland brutality of Reggie Kray to the child killer Colin Evans.

Tim, as an experienced journalist, had seen and reported a number of cases from the other, more public side. He had also worked closely with a number of police forces both in London and throughout Britain on cases concerning child pornography and extreme sadistic abuse.

What struck both of us was that the public perception of murder, influenced perhaps by its fictional representation, was almost completely the reverse of reality. Despite the vast numbers – quite literally thousands – of books and magazines about homicide and its detection, both the fundamental truths of who kills whom, how, and why, and the subsequent humdrum reality of much of the detective's job seemed to have been either missed or ignored.

In part this is attributable to the obsession evident in many of these publications with revelling in the titillating detail of violent crime. Much of this focusses on sexual murder or attacks on women and is, at best, a form of pornography whose aim is to excite rather than inform the reader.

Our primary goal, therefore, was to portray the business of murder as it actually is in Britain today whilst attempting to steer clear of prurient and gratuitous reporting. But in researching this reality it quickly became clear that it is not merely the public at large who misunderstand the nature of homicide, but the politicians, lawyers and judges whom we variously appoint or allow to dictate its detection and prosecution.

In some cases which we examined, it seemed that the Home Office, the Crown Prosecution Service and the courts had not simply relied on the evidence put before them by the police, but had allowed themselves to be influenced by the alluring fictions of crime writers and film producers, or the prejudices born of a cloistered career.

Quite frequently there was a hopeless confusion as to what might safely be called murder, and what should be written down to the lesser offence of manslaughter.

In part this can be put down to the nature of the offence itself. By definition, the homicide victim is not available to give his or her version of events. This, in turn, thrusts greater emphasis on both the suspect's own account – a version of events in which the victim is invariably portrayed as bearing some responsibility – and police techniques in establishing forensic, witness, circumstantial or confession evidence.

It is sharply ironic – not to say unfortunate – that while the second half of the 1980s saw a dramatic improvement in forensic detection with the introduction of reliable DNA testing, there was a simultaneous erosion of public confidence in the general honesty of Britain's police force. The quashing of the murder convictions in the Guildford Four and Birmingham

Six cases, the disbanding of the West Midlands Serious Crime Squad, and uncomfortable questions over the handling of the Broadwater Farm murder trial all conspired to undermine public confidence in the police.

That this happened in a period which, according to official statistics, showed British criminals moving apparently inexorably towards an American-style reliance on guns, knives and blunt objects in pursuit of their chosen careers, was all the more dangerous.

But perhaps within this situation lay also the seeds of this book and the television series which it accompanies. The Metropolitan Police, no stranger to bad publicity, agreed to allow both authors and film-makers unprecedented access to a working 'murder squad'.

For ourselves we were assured that there would be no closed areas, no subjects 'off-limits' and no control over what we eventually wrote. And so it proved: doors and, more crucially, filing cabinets, were opened for us, with no attempt to hide what lay behind or within them.

Before we began, we both liked to believe that there was little about man's inhumanity to man which could surprise or shock us. Ray, after all, works continuously with men whose sexual assaults – particularly on children – are often vicious and potentially fatal; Tim's previous investigations of child pornography and ritual child sex abuse had left deep and indelible mental scars. But the past twelve months have immersed us in something insidiously disturbing.

It is not the brutal bloodiness of some murders – gory though they are – which is truly shocking, but rather the sheer banality of most homicides. Our overpowering realisation has been that violent death is rarely the product of careful planning, but instead, in the vast majority of cases, the result of a fleeting burst of emotionally-charged viciousness, or the 'logical' end of years of domestic brutality.

For the evidence shows quite clearly that most convicted killers are not professional murderers, but ordinary men and women, living ordinary unspectacular lives until the moment that they kill. There is a very thin line separating the murderous wife-killer from the mundane family man. This is not to belittle the offence, but rather to underline the uncomfortable conclusion that violence is now latent and endemic within our society. Murder is not merely all around us, it is a part of us as well.

Of course, there are exceptions to this drab and depressing pattern – colourful cases populated by characters either truly larger than life, or astonishingly brutal. Unsurprisingly it is their cases which attract the most media attention, frequently spawning a sub-genre of fictionalised accounts in the cinema and in books. In this, at least, art is imitating life.

These cases of serial murders, gangland shoot-outs, sexually-motivated killings and homicides by someone calculating and cool enough to attempt an instantaneous cover-up require of detectives a different approach and level of effort from the more common instances involving domestic violence taken to its ultimate conclusion.

These are what the Romantic essayist and poet Thomas de Quincey described as 'murders of quality'. More than 150 years after his paper, 'Murder Considered As One Of The Fine Arts', coined that attractive phrase, its inherent truth was recognised by the Metropolitan Police.

In 1985 dedicated teams of specialist officers were established, trained to meet the needs of an intensive modern homicide enquiry. They were called AMIPs – Area Major Investigation Pools. This book is an account of the work of one such pool: 4 AMIP, based in the unremarkable South London suburb of Croydon and a typical example of a 'murder squad'.

1
The Business of Murder

We are now dealing with more serious crimes than the busiest precinct in New York.

Chief Superintendent Bernie Davis, Croydon, July 1986

The London Borough of Croydon is a living embodiment of the word 'suburbia'. Stretching across 33 square miles on the south-easternmost border of the capital, it is the physical link between the inner-city grime of Brixton and Lambeth and the commuter enclaves of Kent and Sussex.

It is the tenth biggest town in Britain and, in keeping with other ever-sprawling conurbations, boasts a contradictory combination of mirrored glass office blocks, production-line shopping parades and green belt countryside. It is a town of its time – smoothly prosperous on the surface, rocky beneath. It is also increasingly violent.

The headquarters of the Metropolitan Police (Number 4) Area Major Investigation Pool are located on the second floor of the modern and irregular red-brick Divisional Police station. To get beyond the cramped public waiting room and up the stairs requires a five-digit security pass number.

Once past the impressive security door, however, the overriding and immediate impression is of cramped and ill-planned accommodation for such an apparently important unit. There is one general office, a handful of separate rooms to house the five superintendents and one chief superintendent who comprise the total senior staffing, and a separate secure room behind whose locked doors sits one of the team's two HOLMES (Home Office Large Major Enquiry System) computer suites. It is all curiously low-key.

In fact these limited provisions are the product of deliberate official policy. The Metropolitan Police assigns far more of its officers to routine foot patrols, burglary detection and court-related paperwork than it does to the business of detecting the most serious crime on the statute book.

In turn this seemingly-inconsistent policy is based on apparently sound statistical evidence about homicide itself. The Home Office Research and Statistics Department, which compiles and catalogues all information on the criminal justice system, has repeatedly explained that violent crime is but a tiny proportion of all offences committed in any given year.

The 1989 digest of statistics (the latest available from the Home Office) makes the point:

> The majority of crimes which are recorded by the police are property crimes. Although serious crimes of violence attract considerable media attention, these crimes are comparatively rare and a high proportion of them are cleared up by the police.

The statistics which underpin that comforting statement are stark: of the 3.7 million crimes recorded by the police throughout England and Wales in 1989 just 6 per cent – 222,000 – were defined as violent offences. Of that figure 148,000 (approximately two-thirds) were cases of minor wounding.

Taken together, incidents of serious wounding and homicides accounted for only 4 per cent of the entire 222,000 violent crimes: separated out, there were only 640 homicides. Although this showed a 3 per cent increase on the previous year – consistent with the relentlessly rising figures for all crimes of violence – the Home Office was determined to put an optimistic gloss on the trend. The 1989 'Digest of Information on the Criminal Justice System' explained that:

> The apparent increase in the level of violence in recent years partly reflects the increased reporting and recording of such offences . . . Recent changes, for example in the reporting by women of sexual offences and domestic violence, and in the recording by police of such incidents, have led to an increase in the levels of recorded crime for such offences.

The problem with statistics – and with trend-detecting reports based upon them – is that they depend on the way the raw information is handled. In the case of murder statistics, the artificial categories and narrow administrative definition of the offence helps to obscure reality. But before we examine what are, by any standards, highly misleading criminal statistics, we need to define the crime itself, and understand its historic place in the law.

What is murder? At first glance this might seem an absurd question: surely everyone understands what the crime of murder actually involves?

But astute readers will already have spotted that the Home Office statistics refer not to 'murder' but to 'homicide'. Within that semantic caution lies an enormous tangle of misunderstanding and confusion.

To begin with there is no offence of 'homicide'. That term is simply an administrative convenience for Home Office record management, and can refer to any act of killing, legal or illegal (causing death in self-defence being an example of a lawful killing).

In broad terms homicide generally refers to two quite separate offences of unlawful killing: manslaughter and murder. But what determines whether a particular homicide amounts to an offence of murder is not in practice defined by a written statute law approved by parliament, but instead by the (admittedly erudite) words of a sixteenth-century academic jurist, Sir Edward Coke.

His view of the necessary ingredients to turn homicide into murder has become enshrined in common law - the ramshackle English tradition by which the definitions of offences are shaped and moulded by centuries of individual judgements of thousands of individual trials. Coke's 'law' states that:

> Murder is when a man of sound memory, and of the age of discretion, unlawfully killeth within any county of the realm any reasonable creature in *rerum natura* under the King's Peace, with malice aforethought, either expressed by the party or implied by law, so as the party wounded or hurt etc. die of the wound or hurt etc. within a year and a day after the same.

If it seems curious that so serious a crime should still be defined by an archaic piece of legal journalism, English law has taken the anachronism yet further. The 1957 Homicide Act refines the definition (without effectively updating it) by adding a series of less serious offences of unlawful killing such as manslaughter by reason of diminished responsibility, deaths involving suicide pacts or infanticide.

The intention was to provide a succession of differing levels of culpability for the crime of manslaughter, each generally involving some abnormality of mind which would affect the killer's mental stability. But, as we shall see, so vague and unpredictable is the line separating manslaughter from murder, that these safety-net clauses frequently pile injustice upon confusion.

For murder, then, there is still only the antique Coke definition to guide us. But what does it actually mean, and is it up to the job?

Stripped of the archaic language, murder takes place in English law when a person over the age of 10 and legally sane unlawfully kills someone else with 'malice aforethought'. As a final touch the death, though it need not be instantaneous, must take place within a year and a day of the action which caused it.

We will examine the flaws in this convoluted formula shortly, but first we need to understand how so important a law became so confused. And for that we need to explore the history of murder in England.

The earliest records indicating the development of a judicial notion of murder date from pre-Roman times when the loose and shifting feudal federation of local alliances which then ruled most of England were first invaded then subjugated by tribes of itinerant German settlers.

These Teutonic clans took a relatively relaxed view of homicide: the acquisition of fertile land and ensuing wealth was, after all, more usually pursued via the sword than the ploughshare. Killing within a particular tribe was viewed less seriously than petty theft and easily expiated by paying over a small portion of the offender's fortune – generally counted in sheep, cattle and horses. Part of this embryonic 'fine' was to be paid direct to the family of the bereaved, the remainder to the tribal chief for the common benefit of all the clan – a forerunner, perhaps of the notion of the modern welfare state.

We owe our knowledge of these early criminal codes largely to the Roman historian Tacitus, whose accounts also indicate that the responsibility for prosecuting murderers was left to the next of kin. No tribe benefited from the efforts of a feudal equivalent of the Metropolitan Police: such concepts would not even be considered for several hundred years.

But in this early view of murder as socially unacceptable – albeit to a lesser degree than in the twentieth century – lies the foundations of the law today. Murder was perceived not as a moral wrong, but as a practical problem since it caused financial hardship to the bereaved family – hence the notion of paying compensation.

Almost all subsequent English law has been based on this fiscal approach: it is no exaggeration to say that the volume of law-making on any given offence is directly in proportion to its perceived threat to wealth or property.

As the early centuries developed, and with them increasing

material wealth, so the variety of local statutes and proclamations aimed at protecting property grew rapidly. In contrast, homicide law remained static. By the time of the Norman Conquest the major refinement had been not in the moral view of the act of killing, but in providing security for the payment of any subsequent fine.

Two crude systems of community insurance grew up. The Tithing and the Hundred were similar schemes by which either ten or one hundred local free men stood surety for each other's good behaviour. These rudimentary guilds were compulsory, and based on the idea of self-policing by the inhabitants of any given district. Each of the guilds had a president whose name was used to identify the particular Tithing: a transgression by any individual rendered the entire guild liable for a hefty fine in cash or goods.

In theory the network of Tithings and Hundreds (the latter appear to have operated both as a second-tier guild and as supervisor of the scattered Tithings in their district) covered every free man in the kingdom with the exception of those who had already been outlawed. By the eleventh century the system went by the title of 'the Peace Pledge' and had developed into an embryonic federation of community police forces, with the lord of the manor hearing what passed for trials in his own court.

The punishment for unlawful killing was almost universally still a financial penalty, but the law had begun to recognise differences in what we would now call motive: the guilds in this Norman era had drawn the first distinction between justifiable and accidental homicide, and between those categories of killing and the medieval equivalent of Coke's concept of murder.

This crude judicial system operated for much of the early Middle Ages with only minor modifications to the rules of evidence, and a gradual reduction in the use of trials by ordeal (torture). There is little surviving documentation of society's developing view of the crime, but the word murder was certainly in common currency by the fourteenth century when

Geoffrey Chaucer first penned what would – five hundred years
on – become a cliché in detective fiction:

> Tho' it abide a yere or two or three,
> Mourdre will out, this is my conclusion.

Quite what Chaucer's faith in the successful detection of
murder was based on is unclear. Certainly the years between
the late Middle Ages and the (dubiously-named) Age of Reason
saw the crime of murder develop within the oral common law
tradition, so that by the eighteenth century unlawful killing
had become a serious offence for which death by hanging was
the most common punishment.

But the same fate was meted out for a bewildering variety of
other less dramatic offences: piracy, sedition and theft – even
the taking of a rabbit in a snare – were all commonly 'solved'
with the assistance of noose of hemp, a tall tree and a moving
gallows platform. Murder may have assumed a more serious
place in the criminal calendar, but its punishment was far from
unique.

If the theoretical law of murder developed almost randomly
from medieval times to the Age of Reason, its detection and
prosecution were similarly haphazard.

The self-policing concept exemplified within the Tithings
and Hundreds gradually evolved into a general responsibility
across any given community to 'raise hue and cry' – to discover
a crime, identify the suspect and ultimately to bring him before
the jurisdiction of the local manorial court.

Records indicate that by the thirteenth century parish
constables – unpaid part-time embryonic policemen – were
elected by individual communities to organise and oversee the
'hue and cry' policy.

Some larger cities developed an organised network of paid
nightwatchmen to assist the amateur constables. Behind this
was an obsessive belief that crime only happened during the
hours of darkness. The earliest London 'Watch and Ward'
statute, passed by Edward I in 1285, set out his assumption
clearly. It noted that since:

> many evils, [such] as murder, robberies and manslaughters
> have been committed by night, and people have been evilly
> entreated

a curfew would have to be passed and enforced so that:

> none be so hardy as to be found going or wandering about the
> streets of the city with sword or buckler after curfew tolled at
> St Martin's Le Grand.

This thirteenth-century statute is interesting both for the
evidence that a judicial distinction had already been drawn
between manslaughter and murder, and for establishing the
pattern of statutory law enforcement efforts for the centuries
to come: night watch statutes became the accepted means of
bolstering the efforts of amateur constables and the network of
Justices of the King's Peace.

Elizabeth I passed a refined version of the law in 1585,
George II in 1737, and George III in 1777. It was this last Act
which attempted to create for the first time an organised
network of nightwatchmen, both armed and paid, each of
whom was charged to prevent 'to the utmost of his power all
murders, burglaries, robberies and affrays; he is to apprehend
all loose, idle and disorderly persons and deliver them to the
constable or headborough of the night at the watchhouses'.

But all such laws covered only the night-time hours. During
the day, the jobs of peace-keeper, policeman and detective were
all left to the hapless parish constable. It was not a successful
system.

Given that these isolated and unsupported policemen were
not paid for their efforts, it followed that only the wealthier
members of a community could be expected to fill the post. And
so, for a time, it proved.

But by the early 1700s the increasingly effete English
aristocracy had grown tired of this burdensome *noblesse
oblige*, and had begun to pay so-called deputies to take their
place.

Even this rudimentary system might have worked as an

effective precursor of a professional police force, had it not been for the inevitable economies that stunted its growth. The wages paid to parish deputies were entirely at the discretion of those who had been elected to do the job in the first place. The nature of market forces – a system to which they, as good capitalists, all subscribed – should have warned them that paying a pittance would lead to a lower quality of recruits.

The result was that by 1714 the novelist (and reluctant parish constable) Daniel Defoe was able to note in his essay 'Parochial Tyranny' that many deputies were 'scarcely removed from idiotism'.

Within a hundred years the system would, unsurprisingly, be close to collapse, with constables either too stupid or too corrupt to pursue the murders and organised theft which had become endemic. Simultaneously, the nightwatchmen sanctioned by George III's 1777 statute, had become similarly dishonest: crimes of all descriptions flourished.

Parliament's sole solution was to approve ever more draconian penalties for even the most minor offence. Capital punishment – hanging from a handy tree – became the norm for anything from poaching to serial murder. Still the crime wave rolled on.

The obvious answer was to create a professional police force. But even in the riotous and unstable conditions that affected much of England in the years immediately following the Napoleonic Wars, parliament refused to consider it: between 1816 and 1822, three separate parliamentary committees examined the idea, only to reject it as 'too great a sacrifice' of the Englishman's historic liberty.

Even when, in 1829, this shibboleth was finally subjugated to the reality of overwhelming crime, it was the demands of the new industrial aristocracy for the preservation of their property, rather than the alarming loss of life in England's increasingly violent cities, that prompted parliament to pass the Metropolitan Police Act.

This historic piece of legislation created a paid and professional constabulary only for London. Its duties were primarily the preservation of the King's peace and the protection of property. Six years later the Municipal Corporations Act allowed (but failed to compel) provincial town councils to create and maintain their own police forces – though many elected to employ only a handful of part-time constables little changed from the earlier systems of parish deputies.

Overseeing all this change was the Home Department, the government ministry we now know as the Home Office. But for much of this crucial formative period it seems to have been at best nonchalant, at worst thoroughly neglectful, of its duty to supervise and regulate the new police forces.

And as with the police, so with the law itself: it is a measure of the confusion surrounding the crime of murder that successive Home Secretaries of the period continued to act as bounty-paying private law enforcers in individual cases of homicide.

Magistrates throughout the country began by-passing the nascent police forces and looking instead to Whitehall in the expectation that it would underwrite substantial rewards offered for the arrest of any given murder suspect. Such applications were commonly granted by the Home Department.

Typical of this confusion of roles and duties was a case in 1836 in which a killer called Armstrong, whilst serving as a sailor in the Navy, made a written confession to murdering a man in South Shields. The confession was sent from the ship to the Admiralty, which promptly passed it to the Home Department.

Instead of merely forwarding it to the local police, the Home Secretary, Lord John Russell, took on himself the role of bounty-paying crime hunter: when Armstrong's ship reached Portsmouth it was Russell who arranged for someone to identify and arrest him by arrangement not with the local police but with the magistrate. 'Lord John Russell,' the Home Department wrote, 'will provide for the payment of the coach hire there and back and for the personal expenses of such a person at the rate of seven shillings per day, not exceeding eight.'

This extraordinary privateering by the Home Secretary was typical of both the period and the activities of the Home Department. The early years of organised policing were marked by incompetence, ignorance and complacency within Whitehall: the Home Department was happy to do as little as it could possibly get away with. The result, exacerbated by the increasingly unsanitary conditions within Britain's burgeoning industrial cities, was ever-increasing crime. Life was cheap, murder commonplace.

It was not until 1878 that the Metropolitian Police formed its first Criminal Investigation Division. Although there had been a minimal 'Detective Branch' within the force from 1842, and some provincial forces had followed suit in the ensuing years by seconding one or two officers for investigative duty, there is little evidence that they enjoyed much success.

In their defence it has to be said that the standard tools modern detectives take for granted – fingerprinting, intelligence databases, forensic pathology and scene-of-crime photography – were all young, or undiscovered, sciences. Team work was virtually unheard of, especially between neighbouring forces, and all that distinguished these early investigators from their uniformed counterparts was a bag of plaster of Paris (to make moulds of footprints) and an occasional network of local informers.

The Division did not have an auspicious start in life. In the months prior to its formation three of the four chief inspectors in the former Detective Branch were tried and convicted at the Old Bailey for corruption. Even in the new CID the quality of recruits was frequently – and publicly – criticised, and the initial force of 250 bowler-hatted detectives became, for a time, the object of ridicule and scorn.

There is a curious parallel to be observed in this period between crime in fact and fiction. The modern public obsession with murder in books, films and magazines began in these late Victorian years. This was the era of the 'penny dreadful' novel in which homicide, either intricately cunning or explicitly gory, was celebrated and raised to a form of popular art.

And as in fiction, so in fact: these same years saw the rise of the classic English murder. The criminal records for the years from 1800 onward are littered with middle-class poisoners and bloodthirsty knife-wielders, all reported with loving attention to detail in the daily newspapers. Murder had caught the public imagination.

This explosion of literary homicide, at a time when the Metropolitian Police's own detectives were widely viewed as unable to detect the most simple burglary, might be written down to mere coincidence were it not for the deliberate blurring of boundaries by the fiction writers themselves.

That most famous of fictional detectives, Sherlock Holmes, made his first supercilious appearance in print in 1887. This was the CID's 'Cinderella period' within the police, and Conan Doyle's creation captured the popular mood of intense frustration with its inability to conduct thorough and successful investigations on any scale.

The fictional representation was, if anything, over generous. Alone among the major European nations English detective work remained in the dark ages. Scientific crime detection – the forensic examination of blood, hair and scenes of crime which Conan Doyle's Sherlock Holmes stories led the public to believe was both proper and possible – was virtually non-existent in reality.

In France, anthropometry, a crude system of criminal identification based on geometric facial measurements, had been established within the Sûreté by Alphonse Bertillon. In Austria a magistrate named Hans Goss was setting out for the benefit of his colleagues the principles of empirical crime detection employed in his district. In Italy and even across the Atlantic in Argentina, work was well under way in developing reliable scientific aids for the modern investigator. In England alone policemen went about their work in exactly the same manner as their semi-amateur predecessors had in the two previous centuries.

True, it was in Victorian London that the science of fingerprinting was first conceived by Francis Galton from the realisation that no two prints were the same. But petty jealousies and bureaucratic inertia – that staple ingredient of all British public life – ensured that Scotland Yard would not benefit from a Central Fingerprint Branch until 1901.

While the science of detection was on a slow track, crime increased dramatically. The later years of the nineteenth century saw all the evils of the industrial revolution – a mass exodus from countryside to cities, poor housing, bad sanitation, unemployment and cheap drink – combine to produce in London, as in all major conurbations, a state of constant lawlessness. Inevitably, and partly due to the lingering reliance on capital punishment for a catholic collection of crimes, murder headed the list. It was, quite simply, worth the risk of killing a witness to your robbery given the same penalty for both offences and the famed inadequacy of the CID (Criminal Investigation Division).

In polite society as much as in the criminal 'rookeries' of Victorian London the popular perception was of a detective division quite unable to do its job. This mood reached its apogee in 1888 with the first major recorded serial murderer: Jack the Ripper.

The Whitechapel murders provoked a wave of public panic which mirrored – but exceeded – that caused by a similar set of unsolved killings in the same area seventy-seven years earlier. The Ripper killings, however, proved a more potent symbol of the CID's shortcomings. Even Queen Victoria entered the acrimonious debate with a terse telegram from Windsor which read:

> The Queen fears that the detective department is not so efficient as it might be.

Nonetheless, those last years of Victoria's reign saw the beginnings of progress in the development of techniques to detect crime.

In 1892, partly prompted by the failures of the Ripper investigation, which in turn had shown up an administrative *impasse* between the Metropolitan Police Commissioner and

the Home Secretary, the Home Office began to interest itself in
the science of crime.

Its first act was to purchase 'all proprietary rights' to a new
system of taking casts of footprints – a method said to be
considerably superior to the traditional bag of plaster of Paris,
but which still required an array of cumbersome equipment
including a copper-bottomed kettle, resin and wax. Pleased
with this radical advance, the Home Office issued a circular to
all police forces recommending an updating of their forensic
cupboard.

At the same time it had begun to consider the creation of a
central system of 'Bertillonage' – the anthropometric classification of known criminals by their cranial characteristics.
Bertillon had proved to a somewhat sceptical Sûreté that the
technique worked and could dramatically cut the number of
unsolved offences committed by the itinerant French criminal
community. The Home Secretary, Herbert Asquith, was on the
point of sanctioning an English version of 'Bertillonage' when
the first seminal book on the possibilities of fingerprinting was
published.

We shall consider the importance of Sir Francis Galton's
1892 breakthrough when we examine the advances which
forensic science has made in the twentieth century. But no
small credit is due to Asquith for suspending his decision on
Bertillonage pending a Home Office assessment of the new –
and potentially more powerful – fingerprint technique.

But if the ensuing Central [London] Fingerprint Branch was
to be an almost overnight success, it would not be allied to even
a rudimentary nationwide system of crime detection until the
inter-war years.

Scotland was far from unique in having no fingerprint index
as late as 1908 – an omission which led inevitably to allegations
of rough justice and, in that year, the superimposition of art
upon life. Absurd as it may seem nearly a century later, the
British public had taken Sherlock Holmes to heart, frequently
believing both that the fictional detective genuinely lived at

221b Baker Street, and that he would involve himself in their real-life dramas. Certainly Conan Doyle did little to dispel the image, to the point of becoming a consulted authority on matters of criminal activity himself.

In 1908 he intervened in a Scottish murder case. An old woman, one Marion Gilchrist, had been battered to death with a chair in her Glasgow flat. The motive had allegedly been robbery – a small but valuable piece of jewellery was missing – and a bloody handprint was found on the chair. The missing jewellery – a brooch – turned up in a pawn shop. Some days later a local man called Oscar Slater attempted to sell the pawn ticket for it in his club before sailing for New York.

He was duly brought back to Glasgow where Miss Gilchrist's maid, Helen Lambie, testified that she had seen him in the flat and indeed interrupted him in the act of killing her mistress. Slater was promptly sentenced to death.

Conan Doyle was convinced that the verdict was wrong and strenuously campaigned for a re-trial. It is a measure of the power of his creation that his efforts succeeded. The brooch was discovered to have been pawned some time before the killing; Lambie admitted that Slater was not the man she had seen murdering Miss Gilchrist; the detectives were shown to have pressured her into the identification; and the woeful lack of a fingerprinting technique in Scotland – which could have tested Slater's prints against those on the chair – was exposed to public ridicule.

Conan Doyle's intervention was, of course, timely and certainly saved Slater from the gallows. It did nothing, how-ever, to lower the exalted reputation of his fictional detective creation, and highlighted the profound inadequacy of much of the contemporary efforts. Curiously, though, no one appears seriously to have questioned the sense of the capital sentence in an era when murder was so carelessly investigated.

The early years of the twentieth century saw the Home Office sinking back into the lethargy that had characterised its administration of police work since the reluctant founding of the Metropolitan Police almost a century before.

Little, if any, attention appears to have been paid to the newly emerging science of criminology. It is an indication of the level of comprehension of the nature and causes of all crimes, but of murders in particular, that the standard reference work of the period was Major Arthur Griffiths' *Mysteries of Police and Crime.*

First published in 1898, *Mysteries* is an uncomfortable mixture of the excitable crime reporting familiar to contemporary consumers of the *Illustrated Police News*, and Griffiths' own rambling sociological ruminations of the nature, causes and histories of crime.

> I propose to deal next [he announces towards the close of the first of the two weighty volumes] with the murderer on a large scale. I mean the miscreant who takes life as coolly as he drinks a glass of water, and is no better than the unreasoning wild beast that springs by mere instinct on his prey.
> This is the blackest specimen of the born criminal, the 'throw-back' and survival of the savage, the brainless brute who is impelled to destroy life as a matter of course if the fancy takes him . . .

The key to identifying this slavering sub-human creature, Griffiths informed his readers, was heredity. Police forces, in his educated opinion, should pay great attention to the offspring of known criminals, since an irresistible predisposition to murder, maim and rob would be somehow genetically transferred from father to son (Griffiths is rarely as eloquent on the causes of female offending).

> The preventive agencies [the police] are all the more necessary where heredity emphasises the universal natural tendency [to murder, maim, rob etc].
> The taint of crime is all the more potent in those whose parentage is evil. The germ is far more likely to flourish into baleful vitality if planted by congenital degeneracy . . .

With the benefit of half a century of criminology and psychological evaluation of the patterns of offending, it is easy to dismiss Griffiths' antique opinions as no more than a piece of historical light entertainment – a sort of literary freak show. But so great was the inertia within the Home Office that this bogus 'criminology' was widely read and accepted. That Griffiths was simultaneously one of Her Majesty's Inspectors of Prisons inevitably added authority to his theorising.

It would take the Home Office until 1931 to begin the process of dragging detection and criminology into the twentieth century.

By then the always fickle relationship between the Metropolitan Police and the public of London – alternately supportive and vituperative – had degenerated to an all-time low. The fact that some of this lack of confidence was due to problems caused by the wider ownership of motor cars – traffic jams, road accidents and a thoroughly unpopular 20mph speed limit – was hardly the fault of the CID. Nonetheless, morale was at rockbottom, and the need for a review obvious. In 1931 Lord Trenchard was appointed Commissioner, with a clear brief to modernise all aspects of policing in general, but the practice of detection in particular.

In fairness, the Home Office had already made a brave stab at solving the problem. It had sponsored and backed a report proposing the establishment of a national police college which would train detectives in precisely the investigative skills which they so woefully lacked.

But there the effort ended: the Home Office saw the report as a clever means of appeasing the increasingly vocal Police Federation, formed in 1919, by offering the prospect of a training-based career structure. Sir Arthur Dixon, who wrote it, had rather more ambitious – and indeed relevant – plans. He saw the college expanding to become a national centre for criminological research. In taking this line he was proposing a wider understanding of what the researcher Patrick Colquhoun had called 'the science of policing'. That Colquhoun had promoted this concept at the end of the eighteenth century was an indication of the slow rate of progress.

Dixon's visionary proposal, remarkably similar to the aims and activities of the modern Police College at Hendon, was ultimately abandoned on the grounds of cost. When Trenchard took up his post at Scotland Yard, he was, by his own admission, 'an old man in a hurry' seeking to transform an antiquated and inefficient service. His subsequent report, published on 3 May 1933, made uncomfortable reading. It revealed that between 80 and 90 per cent of recruits had not managed to progress beyond elementary education and that promotion remained grounded in Peel's 1829 nostrum that senior officers should be picked from the ranks of constables 'from whom little more was demanded at the start than that they should have a good character and a satisfactory physique'.

That such a policy had survived for more than a century was, Trenchard reasoned, 'very remarkable'. He noted drily that it was now 'no longer possible to shirk the problem of how to secure a steady supply of the best brains from every available source' given that the modern criminal had become 'more skilful, more mobile and more scientific'.

The immediate response to Trenchard's bleak report was the establishment of a Metropolitan Police Training School (as opposed to a national resource), the influx of a higher calibre of recruit, and the establishment of a Home Office committee to study the practice of detective work internationally.

In its five years of research the committee visited every police force in Britain, and then matched their experiences and expertise against similar forces in Canada and the United States. It concluded that Britain lagged far behind the rest of the world in the use of scientific aids in detecting crime.

The report emerged in 1938, a year after Trenchard retired as Commissioner. It recommended – and saw established – the setting up of regionally-based crime 'clearing houses' which would act as intelligence and information centres supplying identification details on convicted criminals to all forces; and systematic training courses for detectives together with strict guidance on the advisability of using scientific aids rather than relying on inspired guesswork.

All of which was a distinct advance on the primitive procedures which Trenchard had encountered in 1931. But the Home Office was shortly to act characteristically: many of Trenchard's more innovative schemes to recruit and train brighter detectives were scrapped or watered down after he retired. The Training College closed down during the war, and when it at last re-opened both its intake and scope were considerably narrowed. Never comfortable with the notion that the detective of crime might actually require a degree of intelligence, the Home Office's position was encapsulated in a memorandum which it submitted to a 1948 committee of enquiry:

> The police service of this country depends for its reputation and efficiency upon the character and ability of the ordinary constables who walk the beat.
> No matter how brilliantly qualified a cadre of officers produced by a Police College might be, this would be no compensation for any falling off in the quality of the constable . . .

That the greatest government ministry and the one with sole responsibility for criminal justice policy should adopt such an intellectual luddism is largely attributable to the historic development of the police and of the law itself: both were called into existence primarily as a means of protecting property, and the easiest way of ensuring that protection was to create a system of semi-educated patrolmen. And it is a policy which has survived to this day.

The inheritor of one corner of its legacy sits in a small office in the London Borough of Croydon, constantly straining to make his allotted resources match the demands of criminal activity.

Chief Superintendent Bob Chapman is head of Number 4 Area Major Investigation Pool. Beneath him he has five dedicated detective superintendents, five detective sergeants and six constables trained to operate the HOLMES computer. Any other staff have to be begged, borrowed or commandeered from (already stretched) local CID offices.

Chapman took over from his predecessor, Bernie Davis, in the summer of 1986 – just as crime figures showed that 4 AMIP's geographical patch suffered more serious crime than even the busiest police department in the badlands of New York.

Frankly, we are understaffed. The Home Office itself says that detectives should form 12½ per cent of the entire police force. All the Divisions in the area covered by this AMIP run on an average of 9½ per cent. When we take officers from Division to work on our murder enquiries, we know that quite frequently we will be given trainee detectives. Even if we get experienced officers many of them will never have been involved in a murder before. We have to teach them the rules as we go along. I think we do a bloody good job considering.

2
Murders of Quality

This crime is not generally the crime of the so-called criminal classes but rather an incident in miserable lives in which disputes, quarrels, angry words and blows are common.

Sir John MacDonnell, Dean of the Faculty of Law, London University, 1905

In any given year at least 550 men, women and children will be murdered in England and Wales.† Of those around twenty will die in the A-shaped piece of territory covered by Number 4 Area Major Investigation Pool.

The AMIP stretches from Lambeth Bridge in inner London to Reigate Hill in north west Surrey, taking in communities as diverse as Brixton and Wimbledon, Clapham and Epsom. More than 8 million people live within its catchment area. A distressingly large number have criminal records. According to Bob Chapman:

> In terms of violent and serious crime the London end –
> Brixton, Streatham and Clapham – is the busiest. But
> murder is a crime generally committed by amateurs, so it

---

† This figure is lower than the recorded homicide tally, reflecting police estimates of the number of cases which are ultimately 'written down' from murder to manslaughter.

isn't confined to the inner city areas. We regularly get
called to cases in middle-class suburbs like Wimbledon and
Croydon.

Murder, like all violent crime, has been steadily increasing
since the end of the Second World War, when an annual
homicide rate of 250 deaths per year was considered
shockingly high. Official Home Office statistics seem at first
glance to suggest that the expansion of murder is slower
than, say, that of violent sexual offences.

But beneath that apparently comforting veneer lies an
unpleasant indication that, if anything, the trend within
society is for more of us either to want, threaten, seek to or
succeed in killing another human being.

Homicide statistics for 1990 showed a 5.5 per cent increase
on the previous year, with 676 men, women and children
being unlawfully killed. In turn the 1989 statistics had
shown a 3 per cent rise on the 1988 figure.

In addition to those successful bids to end another's life,
477 people were charged and convicted with attempted
murder, and 4,160 with threatening or conspiring to murder.
On top of that 8,921 adults were sentenced for more serious
acts of wounding which potentially endangered the victim's
life. In the four years between 1986 and 1990 this category
alone had risen by more than 2,300 separate convictions.

Bob Chapman argues:

The problem is that surgeons are getting better at their
jobs. Whereas a few years ago a knifing would typically
lead to the victim's death, these days doctors are more
skilled at putting the pieces back together again and
saving the person's life. Now that's obviously terrific for
the victim, but it does tend to disguise the truth about the
crime itself. And that truth is that the offender didn't
really care whether his victim lived or died when he
attacked them. Society needs to realise what they are
being saved from.

Chapman also points to anecdotal evidence which suggests

that cases which originated as murder investigations, or even murder charges, frequently result in a conviction for the lesser offence of manslaughter. It is impossible to verify what has become part of detective folklore: the Home Office declines regularly to analyse its annual data to identify the number of such 'write downs'. Nonetheless, the Home Office's reassuring annual package of murder statistics clearly conceals more than it reveals.

In part this is due to the nature and interpretation of the crime itself. Although Coke's common law definition of murder is still universally applied, it has been modified and refined by subsequent statutes.

The Homicide Act of 1957 is the most important of these, and attempts to set some codification on the tradition, which had developed in the years since Coke, of splitting murder into two elements: the *actus rea*, and the *mens rea*.

Perhaps only in England could a modern statute, aimed at clarifying a sixteenth-century definition, rely on a language which had been dead for a thousand years. Nonetheless, the two Latin phrases remain the standard test for lawyers weighing up the evidence in homicide cases.

Actus rea means, quite simply, the physical actions involved in the murder. So, paraphrasing Coke's definition, these are unlawfully causing the death of another human being, and death taking place within a year and a day of the act which led to it.

If this sounds relatively straightforward, an entire library of case law has grown up around this question of causation. How closely do the death and the assault need to be linked? Could other intervening factors have played a significant part? Questions like these are of more than mere academic interest: defence lawyers routinely use them to challenge murder charges or convictions.

Nor is this a new phenomenon: the years between 1830 and 1840 saw a flurry of cases – particularly involving apparent infanticide – which turned on this 'rule of remoteness'.

The classic case, still taught to law students more than

eighty years later, was R. *v.* Dyson, which reached the Court of Criminal Appeal in 1908.

Dyson was an undoubtedly violent man with a propensity to explain his instructions and demands with his fists. In November 1906 he beat his son unconscious and fractured his skull. In due course he was jailed for four months by his local magistrates, but on his release he again beat the boy severely, bruising his head and face. Within a year his son contracted traumatic meningitis and died.

The Metropolitan Police charged Dyson with causing the boy's death. The last bout of facial bruising had, of course, disappeared by the time of death, but there was clear evidence of the fractured skull from 1906. Medical evidence introduced at the trial made it clear that this had been the main cause of death, accelerated by the subsequent violent beatings in 1907.

The problem with all this was that the boy had not died within a year and a day of the main *actus* which led to his demise – the fractured skull – and therefore, under Coke's archaic definition, Dyson could not be guilty of any act of homicide. Lord Alverstone, quashing Dyson's conviction in the Court of Appeal, rammed the point home.

> Whatever one may think of the merits of such a rule of law, it is undoubtedly the law of the land that no person may be convicted where the death does not occur within a year and a day after the injury was inflicted, for in that event it must be attributed to some other cause . . .

Whatever the implications of Lord Alverstone's point – that 'the rule of remoteness' was effectively letting violent killers walk free – legislators have felt able to ignore it ever since. The Criminal Law Revision Committee – the government's standing reform think-tank for all matters legal – decided, in its 1980 report, that the rule should stay, since 'it would be wrong for a person to remain almost indefinitely at risk for prosecution for murder. A line has to be drawn somewhere, and in our opinion the present law operates satisfactorily.'

As ever with the English legal system, the point of principle –

effectively a statute of limitations – has been abandoned by the
Home Office in one particular corner of the world of murder. In
1991, in the face of extreme hostility from all sides in
parliament, the government insisted on a retrospective law
allowing the prosecution of suspected Nazi war criminals living
in Britain.

Although their alleged offences were dressed in the dramatic
garb of 'war crimes', the reality was that each was accused of
mass murder nearly fifty years before. In cases like these,
apparently, Coke's 'rule of remoteness' did not apply. It is hard
to see why it survives at all.

If the *actus rea* has caused the occasional judicial headache,
the *mens rea* element amounts to nothing less than a persistent
and vicious migraine.

Mens rea, as all law students are taught, is the mental
element in any crime: the state of mind of the offender at the
point where he commits his offence. In murder this comes down
to three separate elements within Coke's antique definition:
how 'sound' is his mind, is there 'malice', and was there
'aforethought'?

That, at least, is the theory. But this being English law – and
common law rather than law enshrined in any statute – the
legal meaning of the words quoted above bears no resemblance
to normal everyday usage. According to Dr Barry Mitchell,
senior lecturer in law at Coventry Polytechnic:

> The term 'malice aforethought' is very misleading. For a
> homicide to be classified as a murder there doesn't have to be
> any malice in the sense of spite or ill-will, and the so-called
> 'aforethought' can be a matter of micro-seconds rather than
> the careful planning it seems to imply.
>
> What that means is that even in the case of a caring and
> decent person who agrees on the spur of the moment and out
> of compassion to help in a mercy-killing of a friend or relative
> in chronic pain, the law says there may well be sufficient
> 'malice' for it to be murder.

Much of this confusion has grown up because murder has never
been defined in a written statute law, so that its meaning and

requirements have been shaped by the views of judges across the past two centuries.

The 1957 Homicide Act did attempt to rationalise the notion of malice, but still managed to leave intact the word itself and therefore only tinkered with the edges of the problem.

According to the Act, there are two types of malice afore-thought: express and implied. For express malice the police have to prove in court that a defendant actually intended to kill his or her victim. Implied malice usually boils down to an intention to cause grievous bodily harm with some added notion that circumstances have to have existed that meant death or very serious injury would follow from the actions involved.

This so-called 'aimed act' rule (the defendant has to have aimed at doing something in circumstances which might lead to death or serious injury) is a nightmare to apply. Case after case has gone through the appeal courts and finally to the House of Lords for semantic interpretation of a single word in a previous judgement or in a defendant's statement. It is, frankly, a lottery.

The classic example of this confusion – and typically the case by which most modern appeals are measured in the courts – was R. *v*. Hyam.

The defendant, Ms Hyam, was accused of the murder of two young girls, the daughters of her rival in love, a Mrs Booth (it is a curious aspect of English law reporting that the courts rarely trouble to record the first names of those who come before them).

The women's mutual lover had discarded Ms Hyam for the charms of Mrs Booth, and had announced their intention to become engaged. Ms Hyam was, not unnaturally, upset and extremely jealous: in a bid to frighten her rival away from the locale she went to Mrs Booth's home in the early hours of the morning and poured petrol through the letterbox. After stuffing newspaper through as kindling, she then dropped a lighted match on the pyre.

Mrs Booth managed to escape from the burning house, but her two daughters were asphyxiated by smoke and died. Ms

Hyam was charged with their murder, convicted by a jury at Crown Court, and began a lengthy series of appeals. These culminated, in 1975, in the House of Lords, the ultimate court of appeal in Britain.

Reading transcripts of their Lordships' judgements is generally an unsettling occupation. By the time a case reaches the distinguished panel of judges who are known as 'The Law Lords' all humanity has been squeezed from a set of circumstances originally involving an all-too human tragedy.

Their judgement in the case of Hyam was typical. It was based solely on interpretation of other judgements in which the meaning of seemingly simple words like 'malice' and 'aforethought' had been defined, redefined, split artificially and defined anew, until they cease to have any relevance to everyday life or their normal meanings.

The five Law Lords who considered Ms Hyam's appeal did so not on the basis of what she had done, but on the basis of what the trial judge had said to the jury in his summing up. If Ms Hyam's lawyers could prove to the judges' satisfaction that he had misled them, she might have her conviction quashed and walk free. That she had, without doubt, caused the death of two children would be neither here nor there in this topsy-turvy world of English law.

The trial judge, Mr Justice Ackner, had directed the jury with the following words:

> The prosecution must prove, beyond all reasonable doubt, that the accused intended to kill or do serious bodily harm to Mrs Booth, the mother of the deceased girls.
> If you are satisfied that when the accused set fire to the house she knew it was highly probable that this would cause death or serious bodily harm, the prosecution will have established the necessary intent. It matters not if her motive was, as she says, to frighten Mrs Booth.

The Law Lords rejected Ms Hyam's appeal against her conviction by a majority of three or two. She had argued – through her lawyers, since the paying customer is never allowed to make an appearance before the Law Lords – that even if she had been aware of a 'highly probable' consequence of serious bodily harm arising from her actions, this did not amount to an intent to commit murder.

The Law Lords decided, by a majority of three to two, that Coke's 'malice aforethought' meant an intention to kill or cause grievous bodily harm. Which might have settled the matter once and for all were it not for the fact that a transcript of the judgement showed that all five appeared to have different versions of the meaning of this attractively neat phrase.

The Hyam case has, in a way that is typical of the shambolic functioning of common law, produced a definition of the mental element necessary for murder which has never been sanctioned by parliament and which is still subject to endless legal argument because the five most distinguished judicial brains of their day could not make their minds up on the meaning of six simple English words.

Not without reason do Bob Chapman's officers – and their colleagues throughout every police force in England and Wales – keep a mental register of 'good judges' and 'bad judges'. Taking even the most carefully-detected murder case to court remains a gamble because the law itself is unclear and because judges constantly attempt to redefine it.

Ms Hyam's case also demonstrated both of the eternal truths of murder cases – that it is committed by and large by enthusiastic amateurs with (leaving terrorism aside) only two real motives: sex and money.

A careful study of the statistics to discover who actually kills whom and why shows that the biggest single category is homicide by family or friends. Nearly half of the 230 women unlawfully killed (on average) every year die at the hands of their husband or lover; another 20 per cent are done to death by members of their family – disturbingly frequently by their own children; less then 20 per cent are murdered by a stranger. The home is, quite simply, the most likely place for a woman to die violently.

For men the picture is slightly different. The biggest single categories are friends and strangers – each accounting for one-third of the average 340 male homicides per year. Only 10 per cent are killed by their wives or lovers; 15 per cent by their families.

These figures accurately reflect the nature of a male-dominated society: despite the increase in women working outside the home, the stereotypical family where the husband goes to the office and the wife does not is the most common marriage arrangement. In turn that means that men have more contact with people they do not know well, thereby increasing their statistical chances of dying at the hands of a stranger.

But taken together it is family life and its related stresses and strains that acount for the largest number of unlawful killings. Not all of those will ultimately be recorded as murders. The flip-side of the *mens rea* coin is the reduction of murder to manslaughter where some of the mental elements are missing. Since this frequently is seen to operate in an arbitrary and unjust way, we need to understand what separates the two offences.

In theory the test for determining whether a killing was a murder or a manslaughter is quite straightforward. A homicide which otherwise fulfils all the mental and physical elements of murder will only be reduced to manslaughter if the defendant was provoked or suffered from diminished responsibility. Within that seemingly-simple phrase, however, lies a wealth of inconsistency and confusion.

Section 3 of the 1957 Homicide Act sets out what parliament meant by the notion of provocation:

> Where on a charge of murder there is evidence on which the jury can find that the person charged was provoked (whether by things done or things said or both together) to lose his self-control, the question whether the provocation was enough to make a reasonable man do as he did shall be left to be determined by the jury; and in determining that question the jury shall take into account everything both done and said according to the effect which, in their opinion, it would have had on a reasonable man.

This clause uses a formula standard to much legal draught-manship and goes by the general nickname of the 'Clapham Omnibus' test. (When this test was first enunciated by a judge in the 1920s the average reasonable man was deemed to spend a considerable portion of his waking day sitting on public transport in the South London suburb.)

The Act quite sensibly left the administration of this test to the jury. Under English law the twelve men and women picked to reach a verdict are the sole arbiters of the facts in the case. But English legal tradition being dominated by the common law – itself formed from the opinions, prejudices and decisions of almost exclusively elderly male judges – this independence has been gradually whittled away.

The excuse for this has been that, under the common law which prevailed before the Act, a judge had supplied a rather better defined version of the type of provocation involved, and the necessary effect it had, for the plea of manslaughter to succeed.

The formula invented by Mr Justice Devlin in a 1949 murder trial was substantially the same as the wording of the Act that was intended to supercede it – except that it insisted that the provocation must cause a 'sudden and temporary loss of control'.

This limiting phrase appears nowhere in the Homicide Act, and it is a measure of the power of judges to make up the law as they go along that it has survived the statutory attempt to make it extinct. Its effect has been devastating.

Each year a trickle of cases reach the courts where a husband charged with killing his wife pleads the special defence of provocation on the grounds that his life was made intolerable by constant nagging. In general such pleas, heard with a depressing inevitability by male judges well into their later years, tend to succeed. The so-called 'hot blood' test is applied and found fulfilled.

In contrast it is very rare for a woman charged with killing her husband to plead provocation successfully. The latest comparative Crown Prosecution Service statistics show that nearly 40 per cent of women who killed their partners were convicted of murder rather than manslaughter; for men the figure was 25 per cent. In November 1991 the Home Office released research which appeared to show precisely the reverse of this pattern. Yet other Home Office research shows that a history of brutal and regular beatings frequently precedes the woman's final decision to end the life of her tormentor.

Women's groups argue that the provocation defence simply does not take account of the reality of domestic violence: most women victims of long-term battering feel powerless against an attacking spouse, and are in effect forced to 'plan' – however vaguely – a means of ending their ordeal.

This powerlessness has its roots in both the general physical inequality of strengths and in the abused woman's lack of self-belief after years of brutal treatment by her husband or lover. In short, although these women are provoked – and their pleas should be allowed under the Homicide Act – the insistence of judges in sticking to their common law tradition of demanding 'sudden and immediate loss of control' means that they are denied the protection lavished on men who kill nagging wives.

In July 1991 this was thrown into sharp relief in the case of Sara Thornton. Mrs Thornton, a 35-year-old wife and mother from Warwickshire, had previously been convicted of the murder of her husband with a sharp knife on 14 June 1989.

It was common knowledge that Malcolm Thornton was both an alcoholic and a brutal bully. When he died he was on bail for assaulting Sara in one of many drunken rows: he had, on that occasion, knocked her unconscious.

Much play was made, at Sara Thornton's trial, of the fact that she was herself mentally unstable and that she had been married before to another abusive husband. The judicial system's ignorance of the effects of early abuse on both girls and boys was demonstrated when it failed to pick up the pattern in Sara Thornton's life: as is common with women who have experienced early abuse, she was attracted to men who would, ultimately, repeat that abuse over and over again.

She had left her first husband, taking their daughter Luise, and had met Malcolm Thornton in 1987, marrying him a year later after he had spent time in a detoxification clinic to control his drinking. On the night of the killing, Sara returned from the local pub to find her husband sprawled, drunk, on the sofa. Earlier she had written 'Bastard Thornton I hate you' in lipstick on the bedroom mirror. It was hardly an unreasonable sentiment: Malcolm Thornton had warned his wife that he intended to kill Luise.

Sara Thornton told the court that she first looked for her husband's truncheon – he was an ex-policeman – as a defensive weapon against another anticipated attack, but when she failed to find it she picked up, and sharpened, a kitchen knife. She then tried to wake him and suggested he come to bed. He mocked her, saying he planned to kill her while she was asleep. Sara Thornton stabbed her husband once in the stomach: the blow killed him.

Theoretically, the Homicide Act provided her with a provocation defence: the provocation itself can be verbal or physical, so long as the reasonable man sitting on the Clapham Omnibus would feel the same. It is hard to think that the eponymous public transport commuter would not have felt Sara Thornton's actions reasonable: she had, after all, been treated to enough of her husband's violence to fear that he might well carry out his promises to kill either her or her daughter, or both.

But her plea was rejected and she was convicted of murder. The case arrived at the Court of Appeal in July 1991. It too rejected the plea of provocation: Lord Justice Beldam summed up their Lordships' reasoning:

> There are many unhappy and indeed miserable husbands
> and wives. That is a fact of life . . . On the whole it is hardly
> reasonable to stab them fatally when there are other
> alternatives available like walking out or going upstairs.

The Homicide Act might as well not have been passed in 1957: judges routinely ignore it to reach verdicts based on their own prejudices. On the day Sara Thornton's appeal was rejected – and she faced the mandatory life sentence for murder – a man who killed his nagging wife after momentarily losing his patience successfully pleaded provocation. He was convicted of manslaughter and received a suspended sentence.

The second 'special defence' which can reduce a charge of murder to one of manslaughter is frequently no better understood: 'diminished responsibility' is intended to separate cold-blooded deliberate homicide from killings caused by a defendant's mental disturbance.

The concept was introduced by the 1957 Homicide Act. Section 2 (1) states:

> Where a person kills or is party to the killing of another, he shall not be convicted of murder if he was suffering from such abnormality of mind (whether arising from a condition of arrested or retarded development of mind or any inherent causes induced by disease or injury) as substantially impaired his mental responsibility for his acts and omissions in doing or being a party to the killing.

Three years later, the then Lord Chief Justice, Lord Parker, redefined what the statute had already defined. Abnormality of mind, he decided, meant:

> a state of mind so different from that of ordinary human beings that the reasonable man would term it abnormal. It appears to us to be wide enough to cover the mind's activities in all its aspects, not only the perception of physical acts and matters and the ability to form a rational judgement whether an act is right or wrong, but also the ability to exercise will power to control physical acts in accordance with that rational judgement.

Parker's new version of the abnormality test was significantly different from that envisaged by parliament when it passed the 1957 Homicide Act. The Lord Chief Justice's definition strays into the arena of genuine psychological illness – madness or insanity in everyday terminology – as opposed to the refusal to control irrational urges – simple badness.

That this distinction already existed in law in the umbrella defence of insanity appeared not to matter: it introduced a moral rather than clinical test and gave judges the scope to rely on their own prejudices when determining whether to allow a plea of diminished responsibility. So recent judgements have held that alcoholism and habitual drug abuse can be factors in allowing the plea – but generally only where there is evidence of physical damage to the brain or where the addiction is so strong that the defendant's judgement was grossly impaired.

Of course, in reaching their decision, judges at all levels are provided with expert testimony from doctors and psychiatrists. But a close study of recent case law shows that in at least 13 per cent of cases the medical experts called in to give evidence disagreed on either the very presence of mental abnormality or whether it was so severe as to have substantially impaired the defendant's mental responsibility. In one classic example, an independent psychiatrist reported to the court that he saw 'no indication to raise a consideration of diminished responsibility' while a prison doctor wrote of the same killer at the same time, 'I would be prepared to say that his responsibility was substantially diminished.'

The result has been a system of Heath Robinson justice where the verdict on a killer's mental stability can be as much determined by the public's outrage at his offences as the reality of his abnormal mind. The refusal to allow a plea of diminished responsibility by the Yorkshire Ripper, Peter Sutcliffe, was perhaps the most obvious example of this process at work.

The public confusion which this has yielded is particularly hard for police officers to handle. Local response to their efforts in detecting or prosecuting murders can depend on the degree of sympathy the public feels for a defendant, and – more crucially – on the widespread misunderstanding of the notion of madness.

Many of the more serious homicides – murders which form the caseload of AMIPs and are therefore examined in later chapters – invoke a natural assumption that the perpetrator must be seriously deranged to have committed them.

Detective Inspector Peter Elcock, who as we shall see shortly was deeply immersed in just such a case, found this reaction even amongst his own officers.

> There was an assumption that the man who carried out such a catalogue of unspeakably horrible killings as we were investigating must have been mad. He certainly wasn't normal by any ordinary standards, and later on it was chilling just to sit with him.
> But whether he was mad or bad – and that was a subject of some argument in the office – we just had to get on with our job bringing him to book.

If all these definitions and distinctions, categories and subcategories, seem irrelevant to the business of detecting homicide, there is a very real point to the debate. Since the abolition of the death penalty in 1965 there has been only one sentence for murder: mandatory life imprisonment.

Distinguishing between a case of murder and one of manslaughter has clear implications for what happens to the killer after conviction. By the same token, the society in whose name he or she is punished has a demonstrable stake in the courts getting this crucial decision right. Manslaughter generally yields a sentence of less than ten years: with remission the time spent in jail can range from seven years to a matter of months. Suspended sentences are not unknown. The danger exists that severely disturbed killers may be prematurely returned to the communities which provided them with victims unless the 'mad versus bad' debate is carefully conducted. The present shambolic system does little to instill confidence. According to Dr Barry Mitchell:

> There's a widespread view in the criminal justice system that decisions made by the courts don't always accurately reflect the distinctions between murder and manslaughter.
> In other words whether a killer is convicted of one offence or the other is not a matter of strict legal interpretation but is quite likely to represent the court's personal view of any given case.
> Add to this the lamentably confused state of the law relating to malice aforethought and you can see that juries

may well find it difficult to appreciate the exact legal
boundary between murder and manslaughter.
　　For this reason many of those who work in the criminal
justice system believe a single offence of unlawful homicide
would be much easier to operate.

The problem with this idea, as the Criminal Law Revision
Committee found in 1976 when it raised the question of
redefining homicide, was that public opinion firmly resisted the
apparent weakening of the law of murder. Four years later the
CLRC noted in its 14th Report on Offences Against the Person:

> If we were to propose the abolition of the separate crime of
> murder and its incorporation in a wider offence of unlawful
> homicide, many people would certainly find it hard to
> appreciate that the proposal was not meant to weaken the
> law and would be likely to think that the law no longer
> regarded the intentional taking of another's life as being
> especially grave. We recommend that murder should
> continue to be a separate crime.

Behind this delicately-phrased language was a simple blunt
statement: the public likes a monochrome view of murder – a
black-and-white statement of premeditated killings by callous
and hardened criminals. That this perception – an image
peddled remorselessly by pulp crime magazines – is hopelessly
inaccurate, is ultimately irrelevant. For as long as public
opinion wallows in ignorance, the law of murder will remain as
confused and confusing as it has for the past 900 years. 'Most
murderers are amateurs,' insists Detective Chief Superintendent Bob Chapman. 'Very few of them kill more than
once. Most deaths result from domestic disputes.' Chapman is
restating from experience a truth first espoused a hundred
years ago by his fictional predecessor in the art of detecting
murder, Sherlock Holmes. In *A Case of Identity*, published in
1891, Conan Doyle wrote:

> 'My dear fellow,' said Sherlock Holmes, 'life is infinitely
> stranger than anything that the mind of man could invent
> . . . If we could fly out of that window . . . hover over this great

city, gently remove the roofs, and peep in at the queer things
which are going on, the strange coincidences, the plannings,
the cross purposes, the wonderful chain of events, working
through generations and leading to the most *outré* results, it
would make all fiction, with its conventionalities and
foreseen conclusions most stale and unprofitable.'

It was this twin reality – that murderers are ordinary men and
women occasionally capable of extraordinary homicide – that
led to the formation of Area Major Investigation Pools. Bob
Chapman explains:

> Most murder investigations are domestic incidents that have
> escalated. In these cases there's often very little in the way of
> solid detective work needed. Quite frequently it happens that
> a husband will ring the police to say he thinks he's just killed
> his wife or his lover or whatever. In those circumstances
> there's obviously very little in the way of a 'whodunnit'.
> Until 1985 all murders were investigated by local CID
> officers based in Divisional police headquarters. Although
> Scotland Yard maintains a central 'murder squad', it doesn't
> actually do much hands-on investigating of murder in
> Britain. It's occasionally called in to high-profile cases
> overseas, but basically it's a very small branch with
> mostly a statistical function.
> From June 1985 the Metropolitan Police changed the way
> we investigate cases of murder. Eight AMIPs were set up
> with a brief to handle all serious non-domestic murders –
> cases with a bit of 'whodunnit' in them – together with
> anything else that is designated serious crime or ultra
> high-profile within the area.

Number 4 AMIP was the first to be established,
serving as a test-bed for the concept of highly specialised and
streamlined detective teams. The Metropolitan Police's terms
of reference make it clear that in return for this élite status
AMIPs are expected to mop up the most troublesome crime
with relatively limited resources. According to the latest
guidelines, 'serious crime' is defined as:

a) linked crimes or major public disorder incidents

involving crime where at least one of the offences involved
attracts a penalty of life imprisonment.

b) any case personally designated as such by Commander
Operations or adopted by the Area or Force Coordinating and
Tasking Group.

This wide definition can leave AMIP chiefs attempting the
control of very different incidents, each with conflicting
demands on the Pool's time, manpower and resources. So it was
that in 1989 Number 8 AMIP, based in the central West End
area of London, was ordered to handle both the investigation
into the sinking of the *Marchioness* pleasure boat on the
Thames – a disaster which claimed the lives of fifty-one people
and led to two abortive criminal prosecutions plus the threat of
a private prosecution – and the policing of the violent Poll Tax
riot in Trafalgar Square. Simultaneously Number 8 AMIP was
handling its average annual quota of around twenty complicated murder cases.

'Typically,' says Bob Chapman, 'we get cases of homicide
where the situation isn't clear cut – rape, serial crime of
virtually any description provided it is deemed to be serious
and any major public order incident that happens to come
along.'

Between January 1989 and January 1990 Chapman's staff
handled fourteen separate investigations. Ten were murder
cases. A year later and the total caseload had risen to twenty-
seven, and Chapman had given up trying to estimate the
proportion of murders to manslaughters to serial rapes or other
so-called 'serious crime'.

Although the concept of these dedicated super-squads was
sound and innovative, the logistics of their operation have not
been fully explored by the Metropolitan Police. All AMIPs are,
almost by definition, severely overworked and understaffed.

Under Chapman, the permanent detective strength
amounts to just five superintendents, each with a personally
assigned sergeant. Each of these two-man teams can expect to
handle up to five separate murder investigations every year.
Chapman admits:

It is intensive work. My role is now generally that of a manager rather than a detective, so virtually all the difficult decisions fall on the superintendents.

The job can be a real home-wrecker. Murder doesn't obey office hours, and my officers know that. It has happened that they have been called out on Christmas Day, New Year's Eve – just about every special holiday you can think of.

I've got these men – according to our internal directives – for between one and three years. After that they move on to a different job, taking their expertise with them. But in addition to this turnover, each of the superintendents has duties outside their individual investigations: they have to advise local divisional officers on their cases, they have to prepare enormous amounts of paperwork and they are supposed to be training police officers from outside the AMIP in the nature of how we do what we do.

Chapman, like most other AMIP heads, has devised a carefully structured rolling duty roster to patch up the shortage of men. Each superintendent, mostly referred to as senior investigating officers, or SIOs, undertakes a two-week turn of duty as the AMIP 'caretaker'. Nothing short of death or nuclear armageddon obtains a release from the 24-hour day, 7-day week duty.

The caretaker is the first AMIP officer called in to assess a newly-committed crime. In homicide cases divisional officers are expected to assess an incident almost immediately and call in the AMIP caretaker if the circumstances look troublesome.

In turn, the caretaker must assess whether the case rightly 'belongs' to the AMIP. If it does he calls in the 'next in frame' – the first SIO free (or partially free) enough to take on the case. Most SIOs run more than one case concurrently, and it can happen that an SIO is both the caretaker and the next in frame: so tight is staffing on AMIPs that Chapman is forced simply to shrug his shoulders at the extra burden this can impose. 'I can't do anything about it. If you're the caretaker and the next in frame then you've just got to get on with both jobs. If you're filling both roles it's because the other SIOs are completely unavailable.'

As next in frame, an SIO effectively adopts a case from start to finish. When the caretaker calls him he is expected to go immediately to the crime scene to assess the nature of the problem. 'It's a strict rule that whatever time of day, whatever day of the year you've got to go straight out,' explains Superintendent John Bassett. 'I've been called out on Christmas Day before now – you simply have to put all the celebrations and family stuff on one side and go and get on with it.'

'Getting on with it' – even on Christmas Day – generally means inspecting at close quarters the aftermath of man's inhumanity to man.

Bassett – like all other SIOs at 4 AMIP he has at least twenty-five years' experience in detecting crime – has developed a theory about the investigation of murder.

> The first seventy-two hours are crucial. You know at the end of that period whether it's going to be one you solve quickly or whether it's a sticker. And the scene of crime is crucial.
>
> When I get there it should already have been sealed off by the local uniformed lads. I'll go in and have a look about along with my bagman [dedicated detective sergeant].
>
> After that only the scenes-of-crime officer, fingerprint officer, exhibits officer, Coroner's officer, doctor and photographer will get in. Anyone else has to be turned away for fear of trampling all over the forensic evidence.
>
> As far as I'm concerned the Commissioner himself could come along and I would still turn him away – in fact that's happened to me before. The scene must be carefully preserved: I'm absolutely certain that it's impossible for someone to kill someone else without leaving tell-tale signs of what's happened.

While SIOs like Bassett stay on site, the bagman must get back to the AMIP headquarters and set up an incident room. He must then beg, borrow or otherwise obtain enough officers from local CID divisions to staff the investigation. The bagman is viewed as the backbone of the case – constantly monitoring the progress of the enquiry and the mood of the team as the hours tick away. That mood is likely to depend as much on the level of staffing as the initial degree of success. Bassett argues:

We're always understaffed. Each SIO actually needs two bagmen per investigation. Instead you have one who will be working on a number of other cases simultaneously. In theory he should be the scene-of-crime officer. But he can't do that and organise the incident room, so I have to get someone else in to handle all the exhibits.

The men who are pulled in from Division may not have any experience of major murder cases – though they may have a lot of useful local knowledge. They have to join us at very short notice, which causes strains and stresses in their personal lives. The bagman, in addition to running the logistics of the enquiry smoothly, has to keep me in touch with what the team is going through.

By and large AMIPs work extremely well – 4 AMIP boasts a clear-up rate of 94 per cent. But they do so on a mixture of adrenalin and macho camaraderie: it is rare for a woman to be involved in an AMIP case above the level of computer-operator, almost unknown for an SIO to be appointed from the ranks of female detectives. 'It has happened,' Bob Chapman says, but he can think of only one example, a highly experienced detective superintendent who subsequently moved across to the central Fraud Squad. 'I suppose the life style is not really very easy for a woman, particularly if she has kids. The hours can be very long and very difficult. All the SIOs in my AMIP have been doing this for a long time, so the wives come to expect it. They know that the unsocial hours are just part of the job.'

If the Metropolitan Police has considered the matrimonial effects of the short-staffing of élite squads like the AMIPs, it has never said so. No survey exists examining the incidence of divorce in detectives married to what they themselves refer to as 'The Job'. Nonetheless, marital breakdown is common throughout most police forces.

One less obvious result of the intense pressure, coupled with witnessing the least pleasant side of modern society, is hidden trauma – hidden, because within the macho culture of AMIP investigations, to show such stress is usually unthinkable. Almost from the birth of 4 AMIP in June 1985, the strains began to build. They would manifest themselves within a year, as the detectives handled their first major investigation. Peter Elcock, now a superintendent at Scotland Yard, was then a detective inspector called in on a case of serial murder.

> It never dawned on me the effect the case would have on some
> of the lads – and they weren't a particularly sensitive sort of
> bunch – so I never sort of looked for the signs. But I found out
> a year later what they'd been going through, and I realised
> just how badly a case like this can burn out a good officer.

The case Elcock was investigating was by any standards a baptism of fire for the new AMIP. It plunged the team of detectives into the Hades of the hidden netherworld of sado-masochistic sex which exists in a section of the homosexual community. More than five years on the details linger like scars on Elcock's mind.

3
The Madness
of Sanity

I could say I feel sorry – but I'm not. I knew
what I was doing; I had a clear mind. So
what's the point of saying sorry?

Michele Lupo, 16 May 1986

Michele Lupo is perfectly sane. Peter Elcock mut-
tered the words to himself quite frequently in the summer of
1986: it was almost a mantra, something that would be true
simply by being said out loud. He was not always convinced.

On 16 May the cause of his uncertainty sat on a hard chair
across the ground floor cell in Brixton police station. Michele
Lupo was 33, a handsome Italian, and quite calm. He was also
candid.

> . . . he said his name was Jim. We went to a basement I had
> been to before and we began to caress. He was quite big. I put
> a silk stocking around his neck and we both fell on the
> ground. I was underneath him and I just kept pulling the
> stocking.
> When he was dead I bit off his tongue. He shit himself, so I
> smeared it on his body and tummy.

Lupo delivered this soliloquy in an even, unemotional tone. He
was quite helpful, volunteering details which would make
Elcock's job of matching confession to scene-of-crime evidence

easier. It was the details, coupled with their delivery, that
worried him.

> I've been in the force for more than twenty-five years. I have
> never come across a case like this or a man like Lupo. There
> was no remorse, no sense of what he had done as wrong: he
> just sat there and said he did what he did, so we'd better get
> on with doing our job.

What Michele Lupo did was decided at the Central London
Criminal Court – most usually known as the Old Bailey – in the
autumn of 1986. He was convicted of four murders and three
attempted murders, and received a string of life sentences.

Ostensibly the case was over – a serial killer caught and
caged: a job well done. But ask Peter Elcock whether he
believes the detectives found all Lupo's victims and a weary
look of resignation comes over his already craggy features.

> No . . . no . . . that is, I don't know. Look, he sat there and said
> he did the four killings and the three attempts. He was quite
> forthcoming about them. But he denied point blank he had
> ever done anything else anywhere.
>
> I admit I have my suspicions. Lupo may have done other
> murders outside London and in other parts of Europe –
> though I've nothing to back that up other than reports of
> unsolved cases from countries where he is known to have
> been, involving a similar technique to his.

Elcock's suspicions, and those of his colleagues, ultimately led
them to request Home Office clearance and funding for
investigations in Paris and Amsterdam. An internal memo
spelt out the problem on 12 September 1986:

> During the course of the enquiries it became clear that Lupo,
> himself a practising homosexual, had travelled extensively
> throughout Europe and, in particular, had strong contacts in
> the more seedy and perverted homosexual clubs in Paris and
> Amsterdam. To this day the investigating officers strongly
> believe that Lupo may have committed other murders.

Elcock and his colleagues were supported by the Director of Public Prosecutions – the precursor of the present Crown Prosecution Service. He backed their bid for formal diplomatic letters of investigating authority – Commission Rogatoires – and finally clearance was granted for an intensive six-day journey through the sordid underworld of European sado-masochistic sex clubs.

The trip proved ultimately fruitless: no new leads, no additional murder charges. Perhaps more importantly, Elcock and his team found no clue as to the reason for Lupo's killing spree. 'It really worries me that we never got an answer as to why he killed his victims. He never explained that. We were just left with an apparently random series of killings with no discernible motive.'

Peter Elcock is an intelligent detective. He knows there are two truths in the business of murder: every killer leaves some clue as to his identity; and there is no such thing as a motiveless murder. Michele Lupo murdered his victims for a reason: it had to be hidden somewhere in the evidence.

That evidence began to build up late in the evening of Monday, 10 March 1987. Kevin Pius MacDonagh walked across Earls Court and into the Coleherne pub at 7.30 pm. It was a lengthy trek from his flat in the North London suburb of Wood Green, but MacDonagh made the journey on average once a month.

Earls Court in general, and the Coleherne in particular, are at the centre of the capital's gay nightlife. Kevin MacDonagh went to the pub less to drink than to pick up a sexual partner.

He had been born thirty-one years previously in Clonmel, County Tipperary, one of six children in an ordinary Irish country family. In 1976 he graduated from University College, Cork, with a BSc in biology and moved to London to study osteopathy. Ten years later he worked in a joint practice in Wimbledon.

Kevin MacDonagh was a 'passive' gay – he sought out partners who would bugger him. In this he was moderately successful, though most of his numerous relationships lasted

no more than a few intense weeks. He was particularly
attracted to tall, handsome European men.

As he sat in the Coleherne that Monday night, he alternately
filled in the crossword in the *Evening Standard* and sipped at
his pint of Tennent's Strong Lager. It was a ritual he performed
on each visit before adjourning to his habitual station at the
back of the pub near the ladies' toilet.

By 9.30 pm he had rejected the advances of one man and
succumbed to the attractions of another. Michele Lupo was
dressed in his regular attire: black leather bomber jacket, blue
sweatshirt and dark blue Levi jeans with a black leather glove
hanging out of one back pocket.

In the complicated sign language of the homosexual community the glove and its position carried a message. It told
experienced observers that its bearer enjoyed the sadistic side
of sado-masochistic sex. Kevin MacDonagh was fascinated.

> I was attracted to him. Shortly after he said, did I want to
> come back with him to his place? I said, yes. We didn't discuss
> sex or anything like that. It was obvious he was gay: we didn't
> need to discuss it. We left the pub, turned left, crossed
> diagonally across Old Brompton Road, then across Warwick
> Road towards the tube station.

Michele Lupo displayed no emotion, no excitement during this
brief walk. He guided his new conquest down a short flight of
iron stairs into the basement of Number 32 Warwick Road.

> It was very dark. I was down there before I realised it was
> derelict. I'm not very sure of what happened next – I know we
> went there to have sex, but I know that we didn't. I certainly
> wasn't buggered and I didn't masturbate.

What happened to Kevin MacDonagh was attempted murder.
Lupo slipped a black scarf round his victim's neck and
strangled him unconscious. He left his victim for dead.

> I remember coming to in this little room. All my clothing was
> in position and my flies done up. I was groggy but not really in

pain. I didn't know where I was at first and I staggered
upstairs.

When Kevin MacDonagh surfaced from the basement in
Warwick Road it was 12.15 am. More than an hour had passed
since he had walked down the narrow staircase in anticipation
of an evening's rough sex. As he staggered on to the pavement
he looked into the questioning stare of two uniformed police
constables.

PCs Steven Lewis and Steven Shipton could not have known
it, but in this chance encounter lay the first tangible evidence of
what was to become a trail of serial murder. To them, Kevin
MacDonagh was just another Irish drunk who had apparently
collapsed unconscious in a derelict basement. Neither officer
gave the incident much thought.

Kevin MacDonagh most likely gave his brush with death a
good deal more consideration but ultimately decided not to
report it to the police. There is a traditional distrust of the
police by the bulk of the London gay community – an antipathy
which is mutually felt by many of the capital's detectives. It
was a lack of trust that would later prove costly.

Five nights later, Michele Lupo returned to the Coleherne. It
was a Saturday and the pub was crowded with gay couples out
simply for a drink, and single homosexual men 'cruising' for
sex. Donald Yorke and Paul Spittle belonged to the former
category: nonetheless they flirted mildly with those on the
lookout for the comfort of a stranger.

James George Burns was 36, and a loner. Born in
Edinburgh, he had left Scotland to join the RAF, eventually
being discharged in his middle twenties after a nervous
breakdown. A gentle, friendly gay, he worked as a guard for
British Rail and lived alone in a small flat in Whipps Cross
Road, Leytonstone.

On Saturday, 15 March he began drinking early. By the time
he arrived at the Coleherne in the early evening he was
extremely drunk, but carried on swallowing pints of extra
strong lager until he became weepy and maudlin. He then tried
to pick up Donald Yorke.

> He started a conversation with me during which he told me
> he had been drinking all day. When I asked him why, he told
> me he was in love with his brother [no such brother ever
> existed]. I told him I was waiting for my lover, and he
> remarked that it was a shame. I asked him why and he
> remarked how he thought I was quite nice. I felt as if he was
> just looking for a bed for the night.

James Burns would shortly find someone to offer him
'accommodation': Donald Yorke had noticed a tall, handsome,
Italian-looking man wearing a black leather bomber jacket,
standing on his own in the pub toilets and masturbating. An
hour later he and Paul Spittle saw Burns and the man climb
into a taxi together. It was only a short ride to the basement at
32 Warwick Road, but it was the last that James Burns would
ever take.

The exact sequence of events that led to his death will never
be known – there were no witnesses other than Michele Lupo.
But at some point, either before he died or after, James Burns's
body was used for a particularly extreme variety of sado-
masochistic sex. He was then strangled with a scarf.

The basement where James Burns died was divided into two
rooms with a connecting corridor. Although derelict it was in
the process of some half-hearted renovation. The work was left
in the hands of an unemployed labourer called George
Thompson. In return he was allowed to sleep rough amid the
debris. Because it was still winter, and because it was the
warmest place in the unheated flat, he, and another drifter,
had set themselves up in the back room.

As was his daily routine, George Thompson got up around
8.00 am on Sunday morning. As he walked through the
corridor he glanced in at the front room: he saw a body, stripped
half-naked, lying with its back to the door.

The police description of the scene inside the front room of 32
Warwick Road is revealing in its detail. Detective Superintendent John Shoemake was the 'next in frame' who
inherited the case. Quickly he organised a photographer,
doctor, exhibits officer and the Home Office pathologist, Dr Iain

West: the murder of James George Burns was to be the first major outing for 4 AMIP.

Dr Stuart Crane, a local GP with a surgery in the nearby Goldhawk Road, pronounced the formal 'life extinct' assessment at 10.27 am precisely. His brief statement to Shoemake's rapidly assembling squad was similarly specific.

> He [Burns] was lying on the foor, partly clothed in motorcycle-type leathers. The body was smeared with what resembled faeces and blood. There was blood over his face and injuries to the left side of his head. I did not move the body to confirm whether or not there were other injuries. There was a metal tube under the body, pointing towards the anus.

A little over three hours later Dr Iain West carried out a full post-mortem on the body. What he discovered yielded yet more clues to the type of killer Shoemake and Elcock would have to catch.

The entire front of James Burns's torso was smeared with faeces and blood, and a distinct hand patterning was visible in the dried excrement. There were three bite-marks on his chest in the region of his right nipple. Part of his tongue had been bitten off, and subsequently recovered from the floor across the dirty and sordid basement room. A ligature had been twisted around his neck and tightened sufficiently to asphyxiate him. There was no evidence that he had struggled at all.

Homosexual killings have a (generally justified) reputation for being extraordinarily violent by the standards of even sexually motivated heterosexual homicide. But the death of James George Burns pointed at something far more sinister than a traditional gay murder. Although savage, these have a classic and definable pattern – generally a frenzied attack on the face and the penis, prompted by jealous rage.

The Burns killing was different: there was an element of organisation to it – the murderer had taken away with him whatever he had used to strangle his victim. Then there was the patterned smearing of excrement – a typical homosexual killer would have panicked and left the body, not stayed to daub it with its own faeces.

The bite-marks around the right nipple, neatly grouped and specifically placed, together with the seemingly deliberate severing of the tongue, simply didn't fit the known pattern of hallmark homosexual murders. There was also the mysterious metal tube to consider.

What would have been merely a bizarre case to begin 4 AMIP's career turned into something infinitely more serious later that Sunday morning. Kevin MacDonagh, prompted by news reports of a killing in the same basement where he had been attacked, finally reported his own lucky escape to his local police. When the report filtered through to Croydon, it was clear to Shoemake, Elcock and the rest of the hastily assembled team that they were now dealing with the first evidence of a serial killer.

The concept of the serial killer has become fashionable in recent years. Novels and Hollywood feature films have celebrated and revelled in fictional stories of mass murder and cannibalism: the 1991 box office success *The Silence of the Lambs* glamorised the notion by giving its lead character, Dr Hannibal Lecter, an aura of sinister sexuality. 'Hannibal the Cannibal' t-shirts became, for a time at least, quite a fashion statement.

The reality of serial killers is, of course, far less attractive. Although there have been serial murders since crimes were first recorded, the term 'serial killer' was first coined in the 1970s by an American criminologist.

Robert K. Ressler started using the phrase because the patterns he saw in a killer's behaviour reminded him of the dramatic film thrillers he watched as a boy in his local movie house. Both were episodic – that is, they formed part of an interlocking chain of events, and viewing of the entire series was needed to make sense of one 'episode'. Similarly, the killer's behaviour dramatically evolved and escalated in much the same way that the film plots would relentlessly turn up the tension, episode by episode. It seemed a perfect description.

Robert K. Ressler is not unique in applying such effort to

understanding the behaviour patterns of serial murderers. He works for the FBI's National Center for the Analysis of Violent Crime (NCAVC), itself part of the Bureau's Behavioral Science unit based at the Quantico Marine Base in the rural Eastern Virginia belt which law enforcement, intelligence and counter-intelligence analysts have adopted as a home base.

Ressler works for what is generally dubbed 'The Psyche Squad' or 'The Mind Hunters'. More formally he is designated a criminal profiler.

The idea of profiling the likely perpetrator of a crime from evidence found at the scene is not new. Its origins are, as with so many modern detective techniques, to be found in fiction. In 1841 Edgar Allan Poe published the classic *Murders in the Rue Morgue*, in which Investigator C. Auguste Dupin demonstrated the ability to follow the thought pattern of a companion as the men strolled through Paris in complete silence.

And, inevitably, life ultimately imitated art – in America, at least. By the mid 1950s the embryonic science of profiling was proving spectacularly successful: James A. Brussel, a Greenwich Village psychiatrist, would shortly leave his mark on the history of criminology.

In 1956 Brussel was consulted by New York police over a series of bomb attacks throughout the city stretching back for more than a decade. The devices were always homemade, always assembled identically and generally followed up by letters ostensibly written by the bomber to the detectives who were desperately trying to end his career.

Brussel analysed the letters and hundreds of pictures taken at the bomb scenes. Finally he theorised that the culprit was of East European origin, between 40 and 50 years old, living with a maiden aunt or sister in the Connecticut area. He had, decided the psychiatrist, a deep psychological hatred for his father, coupled with a strong maternal love (the evidence for this was to be found, apparently, in the formation of the letter 'w' in the bomber's regular correspondence with police).

Brussel informed the detectives that their suspect was paranoiac and meticulous in his personal habits. When he was found, the psychiatrist advised, he would be wearing a double-breasted suit carefully buttoned up.

And so it proved. The man the press dubbed 'The Mad Bomber of New York' turned out to be one George Metesky, a disgruntled ex-employee of the local utility company, of suitably East European origin and living in Waterbury, Connecticut, with not one but two maiden sisters. He was also wearing a neat double-breasted suit when the detectives called in to arrest him. It was buttoned.

Brussel's techniques attracted the attention of a former officer of the San Leandro police department, California. Howard D. Teten joined the FBI in 1962 and spent a good deal of time studying with the New York psychiatrist as well as developing his own approach to understanding the minds of serious criminals.

Teten added Sherlock Holmes to the pantheon of literary figures who were rapidly becoming the patron saints of scientific detection. Conan Doyle's fictional sleuth had two particular messages for his twentieth-century successors:

> Number one, the most obvious thing is probably the correct
> one. And number two, if you've eliminated all other
> possibilities whatever is left is probably what happened.

Throughout the 1960s Teten gradually refined his technique, forever adding data from new cases to his storehouse of information about the pattern of particular crimes. By the end of the decade he was appointed as an instructor in applied criminology at the FBI's then main training division based in Washington DC.

In 1972 he was joined at the Bureau by a former Christian Brother called Patrick J. Mullany, who had devoted much of his subsequent career with the FBI to the study of aberrant criminal behaviour.

Very quickly the pair's classes brought in a flood of new cases – from students at the training academy and from police divisions throughout the United States. The requests were generally the same: would the Bureau's experts cast their eyes over the enclosed data and come up with a profile of the likely perpetrator?

They would, did, and were generally successful. Ten years after Teten was appointed to the training staff, the FBI was regularly called in to profile killers across America. The discovery of the nude body of a 26-year-old special education teacher on the roof of her Bronx house in October 1989 led to a now-familiar approach.

The woman had been badly beaten around her face, her nipples had been cut off and the strap of her own handbag had been used to strangle her. Inscribed on the inside of her thigh was the following message:

Fuck you. You can't stop me.

Detective Thomas Foley of New York Police Department was at first sceptical about the likely benefits of consulting the FBI's new Behavioral Science Academy at Quantico – the institution where the Bureau's nine profilers now worked. Nonetheless, he mailed off a copy of the autopsy report together with photographs taken at the crime scene.

Within a few days he received a description of the probable killer: white, 25 to 30 years old, known to the victim and either living or working nearby. He – the murderer – was definitely male, would be a high school drop-out, living alone or possibly with a single parent. He would own an extensive collection of pornography. Additionally, he would probably have already been interviewed by the police in the course of the investigation.

Ten months later Foley arrested a 32-year-old drop-out who knew the teacher well, lived on the fourth floor of her appartment building and shared a weighty collection of pornography with his father with whom he shared the flat. He had indeed been interviewed in the early stages of the enquiry, but ruled out when it was discovered he had been in a mental hospital at the time of the murder.

Only after the profiler's analysis did the detectives think to check the level of security at the hospital. It proved to be non-existent, with inmates free to come and go as they pleased. Late in 1980 a New York jury decided the young man had murdered the teacher. Foley's boss, Lieutenant Joseph D'Amico was moved to comment: 'The profilers had him so right I asked the FBI why they hadn't given us his phone number, too.'

The secret of the profiler's success lies in careful accumulation of data from a vast number of individual cases, coupled with patient analysis of particular patterns within each category of offence. In 1982 the National Institute of Justice gave the Behavioral Science Unit a grant of $128,000 to build a database of taped interviews with more than 100 convicted serial murderers or political assassins, and then computer-analyse the similarities in each case.

The study was a piece of criminological research unique in the history of detection anywhere in the world. Among those killers consulted were Charles Manson and David Berkowitz, the so-called 'Son of Sam' killer who generally located his victims in lovers' lane locations. Berkowitz's information was frequently vital, according to Robert Ressler:

> He told us that on the nights when he couldn't find a victim to kill, he would go back to the scene of an old crime to relive the crime and fantasise about it. Now that's a heck of a piece of information to store somewhere to see whether other offenders do the same thing.

This approach of storing, and analysis, applying statistical probabilities and Holmesian common sense, has enabled the FBI's 'Psyche Squad' to categorise killers into two broad types: Organised and Disorganised (with an inevitable crossover 'Mixed' category).

If the post-mortem or crime scene evidence indicates that, for example, a sexual killer acted in a controlled, methodical manner from the point of abducting his victim to the moment of the rape or murder – typically by bringing and subsequently removing the murder weapon – then the likelihood is that the perpetrator is an Organised offender motivated primarily by a deviant sexuality where anger has been channelled into rape.

This type of killer is likely, the profilers have demonstrated, to be of at least average intelligence, both socially and sexually competent, and born early into a family where the father held down a steady job but where parental discipline was inconsistent. Frequently the Organised offender lives with a woman, generally drives a well-maintained car, and commonly commits his crimes after experiencing some stressful event.

His victims tend to be strangers and will generally conform to a type or category he has targeted. The Organised killer will frequently take souvenirs from the crime scene – but always in a controlled and methodical fashion. He generally takes a good deal of care to hide his victim's body.

If, on the other hand, the victim's body bears the marks of a frenzied attack, with a sloppy pattern of wounding rather than a neatly grouped selection of injuries, he is likely to fall into the Disorganised category.

The killers in this classification tend to be less intelligent, overtly inadequate socially and sexually, and loners given both to self-delusions and what the FBI quaintly terms 'solo sex'. The Disorganised killer murders spontaneously – but frequently in a particularly brutal fashion – and makes little or no effort to hide the body.

Inevitably these designations are not absolute: the profilers have found that some killers, even some serial murderers, fall into a so-called 'Mixed' category between the two. These men can be seen to alternate Organised and Disorganised behaviour in a pattern that is recognisable as either of the two major classifications.

By 1986 the profiling service had been incorporated into the new FBI National Center for the Analysis of Violent Crime. The Bureau was handling a minimum of 600 cases every year and, by its own estimate, contributing 'significant aid' to local police forces in 80 per cent of them.

The Bureau's success was largely due to the dedication and ability of its nine full-time profilers, but assisted in no small measure by a sensitive understanding of the innate prejudice common to most professional detectives.

In writing up the profiles the FBI steers clear of psychiatric jargon, preferring to couch its assessments in plain – sometimes blunt – English. Officially this is because law enforcement has more need of physical characteristics than a mental profile; unofficially it recognises that most policemen view psychiatrists with considerable suspicion, and their art as a modern form of witchcraft.

It is a lesson British police forces – fragmented into a regional structure and with no federal agency like the FBI to consult – have yet to learn. Profiling in Britain is a largely untried technique: there is no equivalent to the National Center for the Analysis of Violent Crime – though Lord Trenchard's concept of a national police training college might well have closed the gap had it not been strangled by the Home Office.

As a result profiling is spasmodic and half-hearted: when the police consult anyone, they tend to consult psychiatrists or psychologists – most of whom are already working on the defence/prosecution expert court circuit. Their results are generally viewed with deep suspicion by both sides in any subsequent prosecution.†

For John Shoemake and Peter Elcock that Sunday in March, 1986, there was an even smaller pool of profilers to turn to:

> We eventually got one who told us what sort of person would
> have been responsible for carrying out the murders we were
> investigating.
>   He said that the man would have to have known and
> understood what he was doing – that he took a conscious
> decision to kill in each case and that he would have been
> aware of the consequences.
>   The best analogy he could come up with was of a normal

† The main exception to this rule of thumb is in Ray's work with a number of police forces in profiling sexual offenders. In contrast to most other British 'profilers' Ray is not an academic or clinical psychiatrist, instead basing his assessment on the patterns of criminal behaviour evident from his clients at Gracewell. That this matches the FBI approach is not surprising: Ray was trained in profiling by the Bureau.

person who needs to buy something from a shop but can only find a place with double yellow lines to park his car. The ordinary bloke either thinks to himself that he'll park up and dash in and out of the shop – knowing that he could get a ticket and being prepared to risk it – or he drives round till he finds a proper place to stop.

Our killer, so the profiler said, had a more advanced form of logic than the ordinary bloke. He knew that he wasn't allowed to murder people and that if he was caught he'd go to prison for life, but – just like the man who risks a parking ticket for something he wants – he was prepared to risk imprisonment.

But this doubtless intriguing psychological assessment took the detectives no further in physically identifying the murderer. Their sole asset remained a vague and unhelpful description of Kevin MacDonagh's assailant.

In the absence of this vital information, there is only one technique genuinely left open to detectives investigating serial crime: sit and wait. While the motive of the serial killer may seem the most difficult to fathom – and potentially, therefore, makes the job of tracking him down appear impossible – his need to commit the crime over and over again makes him amongst the most exposed of all offenders. It does not, however, make life comfortable for his pursuers or the group he has targeted for slaughter.

For the detectives of 4 AMIP it would be three weeks before they found a new trail to follow: three weeks of interviewing relatives and friends of James Burns and Kevin MacDonagh in the hope of finding a clue to the identity of their mutual attacker.

On the morning of Saturday, 5 April, a new clue was found in a concrete hut beside the railway lines in Ferndale Road, Brixton. It was another body.

Anthony Connolly was 26 and flamboyantly homosexual. He had left school in Newcastle-Upon-Tyne with an A-level in art and a sexual preference for accepting rather than performing buggery. A cheerful, thoughtful and relaxed man, he was not promiscuous by the standards of some sections of the gay community: his friends never detected any overriding interest in sado-masochism.

After studying art on a degree course, he drifted into the catering industry and by January 1986 he was employed as a chef at a vegetarian restaurant in the East End. When its owner, in keeping with the growing public taste for vegetarian food, decided to transfer the business to Soho, Tony Connolly was temporarily laid off.

The lack of a steady wage didn't prevent him from frequenting his regular haunts – the Coleherne pub in Earls Court, the Prince of Wales in Brixton, and Heaven, a gay club situated just north of Hungerford Bridge, in Villiers Street, WC2.

In 1986, Heaven commonly attracted a wide range of gay clientèle. It was, however, particularly popular with 'Leathermen' and 'Queens'. Despite more than twenty-five years in the Metropolitan Police, Peter Elcock was blissfully ignorant of the myriad social, sexual and economic strata into which the London homosexual community voluntarily divides itself. He was about to gain an intimate education.

Simon John Walder, Tony Connolly's flatmate and sometime lover, patiently explained the distinctions in a lengthy interview.

> There are a large number of gay men of all ages who are into leather. This takes different forms. Some people simply like the look of black leather: motorbike jackets, jeans, bike suits, chaps and waistcoats. Others are sexually aroused by wearing these garments, and others adopt this uniform with accessories to indicate to each other a preference for SM – sado-masochistic sex.
>
> This takes several forms including any combination of the following: active and passive oral sex; active and passive anal sex; bondage; physical punishment with hands, canes, belts and occasionally whips.
>
> It is not unknown for gay men with SM inclinations to construct quite elaborate fantasies with each other before having sex. This can involve bondage, humiliation, verbal orders, even such things as one partner urinating on or in the other. It is not unknown for such activities to take place in public parks at night, derelict buildings and even clubs.

Tony Connolly never displayed any predilection for sado-masochism to Simon Walder in the three months they lived, and periodically slept, together. Nonetheless, the sometime chef was the object of a number of such proposals at the Coleherne and Heaven. In part this was due to his adoption of at least some of the leather 'uniform'. He habitually wore a black leather motorbike jacket embellished with an eyecatching display of silver studs – a sartorial message to SM-inclined gays that its wearer might be open to offers.

Tony Connolly had lived on the gay scene long enough to know the confusion he was causing – indeed there is some evidence that he had accepted the advances of at least one sadistic partner whom he allowed to 'fist-fuck' his anus.

At 9.00 pm on Friday, 4 April 1986, he left Simon Walder's flat on the Cowley Estate in South West London, and headed for the Prince of Wales in Coldharbour Lane, Brixton. He was wearing the black leather jacket over a green t-shirt with a handkerchief knotted around his neck. But it was the clothes from the waist down that attracted most attention: under remarkably distressed and severely slashed blue jeans, Tony Connolly sported a pair of shocking pink tights.

Michele Lupo arrived at the pub at 9.30 the same evening in the company of a (platonic) girlfriend and quickly struck up a conversation with a handful of her acquaintances they had bumped into. No one saw him slip out of the Prince of Wales, but Tony Connolly left just before 1.00 am. His last conversation was with the doorman and concerned the pink tights, which had attracted more than their fair share of interest throughout the evening.

There are no witnesses to describe the meeting between Michele Lupo and Tony Connolly. But it is clear that very shortly after leaving the pub both men agreed on a spot of 'quick trade': a euphemism for impromptu and frequently *al fresco* sex.

The main railway line through South London runs for a time alongside Ferndale Road, Brixton. Disused line workers' huts punctuate the otherwise drab landscape of inner-city dereliction. It was to one of these that Michele Lupo led his victim. Once inside both men removed various layers of clothing and began to caress. Within minutes Tony Connolly found a woman's stocking wrapped round his neck and tightening. He died without struggling.

Michele Lupo sauntered out of the hut and clambered back across the rail lines to Ferndale Road. He hailed a black cab and asked the driver to take him to a night club. For the next hour he danced, drank and socialised with no evident concern for the body in the railway hut. At three in the morning he went home and slept.

Two schoolboys found Tony Connolly at 5.00 pm that Sunday. Adrian Power and Shane Hughes were playing on the lines when they peered in through the hut's dirty window. Even through layers of grit and grime the teenagers could see that the body on the floor was uncomfortably still. They also noticed that its trousers were round its ankles, there was a bruise on one eye and bite-marks on the torso. They ran until they found a policeman.

The subsequent post-mortem established that Tony Connolly had died from asphyxiation and that there was evidence of other abuse on his body. The bite-marks, in particular, were curiously placed – on the chest, neck and penis. Additionally, a small bottle marked TNT was found beside his body.

TNT is a brand-name for a chemical substance otherwise known as 'Poppers' and more scientifically defined as amyll nitrate. It is sold in sex shops or via mail order and is particularly prized by gay men for its ability to produce a heady 'rush' of dizziness. The actual reason for this is that the chemical speeds up the heartbeat dramatically when inhaled and is thus extremely dangerous: its homosexual advocates care only that it can create an intense sensation of abandon, especially if taken during anal or sado-masochistic sex.

Because of the nature of the AMIP 'next in frame' structure, Tony Connolly's murder was not immediately handed to John Shoemake, the SIO handling the enquiry into James Burns's murder. However, it – and with it a number of other cases – would shortly fall into his lap.

If, with hindsight, we can see a pattern developing amongst Michele Lupo's murderous assaults, that luxury was not available to 4 AMIP.

The deaths of Burns and Connolly, and the attempt on Kevin MacDonagh's life, were not necessarily linked by anything other than homosexuality and strangulation. Even if the wisdom of extensive profiling had been available, what Lupo did next would have thrown the system out of joint.

At 1.00 am on Friday, 18 April, Stephen McKean climbed the steps between Embankment Station and the Hungerford Bridge. At the top he began walking towards the centre of the bridge.

Stephen McKean was 17 years old, unemployed and very drunk. He had spent the evening sinking into an alcoholic depression at his unpromising circumstances, and by midnight had decided to commit suicide. The Hungerford Bridge was to be his passage into the next – with luck better – world.

To get to the bridge he had crossed Villiers Street and along by the area of Charing Cross railway station known as 'The Arches'. Here, vagrants, the homeless and those down on their luck sleep out in cardboard boxes: 'Cardboard City' was, by 1986, a thriving community of enforced squalor.

As Stephen McKean walked to the centre of Hungerford Bridge he noticed what he took to be a resident of 'The Arches' lying sprawled in the middle of the footbridge. Immersed in his own thoughts of self-destruction, he managed to ignore the vagrant for some five minutes.

When, faced with the prospect of a long and doubtless painful drop, he managed to regain his will to live, he suddenly noticed that the tramp was distinctly still. To his credit he tried hard to revive him before realising that such effort was hopeless. He quickly summoned help.

Stephen McKean might have been forgiven for feeling aggrieved at what happened to him next. He was detained for no less than thirty-six hours and questioned repeatedly. It was

clear from the detectives' approach that they were very
unhappy about his presence on the bridge so close to a dead
body.

But in part Mr McKean had himself to blame. Not merely
was his suicide story viewed with some suspicion, but he
insisted on giving his interrogators a bogus name. The thirty-
six hours spent in the bleak surroundings of a Metropolitan
Police interview room – cold, hard places with an impressive
severity of furnishing – might have been uncomfortable for
him; they could have been vital for the detectives.

There was nothing, in those crucial early hours, to link the
killing of the unnamed vagrant with the nascent series of
murderous attacks on young homosexuals in the AMIP's area.
Only the cause of death was the same – strangulation by a scarf
or tights.

Had the police had the benefit of the FBI's in-depth profiling
they might have attached some extra significance to the only
other remarkable evidence found at the scene. Someone –
presumably the murderer – had gone to some trouble to move
the body: there were drag marks, two feet wide and stretching
for some fifteen yards. It pointed to an Organised killer.

At first sight it would be easy to fall into impatience at the
apparent obduracy of detectives in not linking cases of
strangulation. But John Shoemake and Peter Elcock knew
that death by ligature is an increasingly popular method of
dispatching a victim: only the traditional blunt instrument and
the ever-more popular knife are higher in their cause-of-death
league tables.

And so the death of a vagrant was recorded and a file opened.
It was becoming a busy spring for the new Murder Squad.
Twenty-four hours later Michele Lupo struck again.

Mark Leyland was 22 years old and a little confused. Born in
Liverpool, he had come to London and in April 1986 was
working as a chef at a hotel in Park Lane. His confusion
stemmed from what he would later describe as uncontrollable –
and unaccountable – homosexual urges.

He finished work at 11.30 pm that Friday and, after a brief

drink with some friends, set off in the direction of Heaven. He had no intention of going inside the club; instead he had hoped to pick up a man on the streets surrounding it. One of those was Villiers Street, near the Hungerford Bridge.

> I had read that it was the place to go if you wanted to meet someone. I arrived at Villiers Street and sat down on a seat by the entrance to the underground. Then I got up and started walking, still looking for someone.
>
> I walked down on the footway on the lefthand side and I saw a man walking up the footway on the right. I can't remember who made the approach or what was said, but I do know that we came up to each other and spoke.
>
> I told the man my name was Marco – I didn't tell him my real name because I didn't want him to know who I really was.
>
> He suggested we go to a place that he knew nearby and I agreed and walked with him. Although we didn't discuss what we were agreeing to we were both aware of what was going to happen.

Mark Leyland followed Michele Lupo down a dark and twisting alley and eventually through the broken glass of a derelict and dirty disused toilet. Both men pulled down their trousers, and Lupo pushed forward his penis for the younger man to fellate.

Mark Leyland was never quite sure what made him change his mind, but something prompted him to stop giving Lupo oral sex.

> I remember saying, 'I can't do it', and moving away from him in this small room. He began to hit me hard on the top of my head with his fists a number of times. I don't remember it hurting me at that point in time, but I didn't defend myself. I said 'don't hurt me'; he didn't say anything.
>
> He got out of the window and I was left inside. He came back very soon after and started to hit me through the window with what I thought was a plank of wood. I remember that whatever he had must have been pretty large because he was standing back from the window to push the object through, and was sort of prodding me with it very heavily about my head and face.

I turned away from him and the object; he continued to hit the back of my head. I don't think I called out or said anything and he wasn't saying anything. I think I must have lost consciousness.

Eventually Mark Leyland crawled out through the toilet's broken window and collapsed on the pavement in Hungerford Lane. At 4.15 am he was found by a local beat policeman.

It is hard to resist the belief that, whatever his uncertainty over the homosexual urges which had begun to dominate his life, Mark Leyland knew that the brand of sex he sought that night would be on the rough side.

He was certainly less than forthcoming in his initial statements to police – a reticence, he would say later, caused by embarrassment at the prospect of wider knowledge of his homosexual tendencies. This bashfulness prevented him from telling detectives anything about his attacker, the hut or the sexual comfort he sought that night. It was instead recorded as a particularly vicious mugging, and Michele Lupo remained free and able to prey on other gay men.

Damien Michael McClusky died in the early hours of Friday, 25 April. It is a measure of his anonymity in the world that his disappearance was not reported to police for another three days and that his body was not found until 16 May. Even his age is not recorded in the files relating to his death.

What is known is that Damien McClusky was a likeable and well-liked gay, approximately 24 years old when he died, and originally from Northern Ireland.

He had arrived in London in October 1985 and shortly after began frequenting gay pubs and clubs. He landed a job as a receptionist at the Philbeach Hotel in South West London – a hotel primarily used by the gay community.

In the six months prior to his death, Damien McClusky picked up a number of men for sex – sometimes taking them back to the Philbeach, on other occasions going with them either to their homes or enjoying a spot of quick trade in the open. Among the clubs he went to in search of a sleeping partner were Heaven and Copacabana in Earls Court Road.

At around 2.00 am on 24 April he emerged from Copacabana alone. But before he could make his way back to the hotel, as was his wont after such late-night excursions, he met and was attracted to a man walking along the street.

The men exchanged glances and tacitly agreed on sex. The stranger suggested finding 'a place': Damien agreed. Together they walked around the corner into Cromwell Road. At Number 150 the stranger stopped. The house was covered in scaffolding, half-derelict and half-renovated. He pointed to a basement which had clearly not yet been done up.

The only way in was to clamber along a steel girder and jump down into the exposed room. Both men completed the manoeuvre quickly and pulled down their trousers. They began caressing each other.

It was at this point that Michele Lupo – the stranger who had seemed so attractive to Damien McClusky – began considering his new lover's death. The basement contained an old medical trolley, covered with a white cotton sheet. As the younger man began to fellate him, Lupo decided it would make an ideal ligature. He began to ease it over his hands.

Quickly he wrapped it round McClusky's neck and began to tighten it. His victim didn't struggle, but died with tongue clamped between his teeth in the classic symptoms of strangulation. Michele Lupo adjusted his trousers, looked around, and climbed up out of the basement. He hailed a black taxi and went home to sleep.

By the time Damien McClusky's bruised and decomposing body was found three weeks later, Lupo would have attacked his last known victim, and a noose of evidence would be tightening around his own neck.

David Nigel Cole was frankly lucky. The 30-year-old ticket collector for London Transport was an experienced homosexual who had, by the middle of 1986, restricted both the volume and quality of his sexual relationships as a direct result of AIDS. He had abandoned buggery in favour of oral and manual sex with a relatively small number of partners.

At twelve o'clock midnight on 8 May he left the Wandsworth

council flat he shared with his former lover, ostensibly in search of a beefburger and cigarettes. He bought his late-night meal from a burger bar in Clapham High Street, but instead of taking it home sat on a wall to eat it.

He then meandered down towards Wandsworth Road and past a gay pub, watching with interest as two men emerged and apparently followed each other towards a dark alley for sex. When one pulled out of the arrangement, David Cole was ready to take his place.

> As I approached the alleyway the first man came back out and walked towards me. As we approached one another we looked at each other. As I passed him I stopped and looked back and I saw that he had done the same.
> We both then walked along under the railway bridge and it was obvious there was a sexual attraction between us. I asked him if he wanted to come to my flat and he declined, saying he hadn't got time. We turned left into Wyvil Road and he suggested that we should find somewhere round here. It was clear to me that he meant somewhere to have sex.
> We crossed over towards the lorry park behind Vauxhall station. I can't remember who suggested that we should go in there but we did.

David Cole clearly remembers the beginnings of what was intended to be a brief bout of casual sex. Both men partially undressed before mutually masturbating and fellating each other. Curiously, he felt, Michele Lupo was unable to sustain an erection.

As Cole squatted down vainly trying to stoke his pick-up's ardour, he was vaguely aware of Lupo reaching around behind him for an object in the dark.

> He was no longer touching me with either hand and then there was a sudden movement and I felt something around my neck. Both his hands were behind my neck but I could feel something around my neck pressing against the front of it. I put my right hand up and tried to pull whatever it was forward: it felt like some kind of material.
> As we were struggling he pushed me on to the floor on my

right side and I could feel whatever was around my neck tightening all the time. I tried to pull it away with both hands but I wasn't able to. I then put my left hand up into his face and started to shout 'Help'. The next thing I felt was him biting my thumb: I was also aware of him kneeling on my chest.

I continued to struggle and shout and he then punched me in the face and let go of my thumb from his mouth. Whatever had been around my neck became loose and I remember saying to him, 'You won't succeed.'

He then suddenly stood up and let go of me. As I got up I felt something drop from around my neck to the floor. I looked around and saw that he was standing about eight feet away in the road and looking back at me.

As David Cole continued to yell for help at the top of his voice, Michele Lupo disappeared. But the last lingering glance had been enough: this time the victim would be able to identify his attacker.

But to do that David Cole needed to pluck up the courage to make a complaint to the police. Anxious about their likely reaction to the reason for his presence in the lorry park, he rang the Gay Switchboard 24-hour telephone helpline. The voice at the other end of the phone advised him against reporting his brush with death because the police were likely to give him 'hassle about the sex aspect'.

Considering the efforts Shoemake, Elcock and the rest of the AMIP team were making in warning the homosexual community about a serial killer in their midst – posters in pubs and clubs, together with alerts in the gay press – the switchboard's advice was less than astute. It did, however, accurately reflect the increasing hostility between radicals in the movement and those they saw as their oppressors. Since it was far from uncommon for gay men to be arrested simply for holding hands in public, the detectives were reaping the rewards of years of intolerance and suspicion.

Fortunately, David Cole was made of sterner stuff. He decided to risk disapproval of his sexual habits and rang his local police. He also walked back to the lorry park and retrieved a black stocking from the area where he had been attacked.

Then he reported to St Thomas's Hospital casualty department
for attention to his thumb.

The description of his attacker which he was able to give
detectives later the same day was remarkably detailed. It
would have been enough to put together an accurate photo-fit
of a man wanted for attempted murder. But taking the case
further posed a problem: there was no good description of the
man wanted for the successful killings of Tony Connolly and
James Burns; as to Damien McClusky, it would be another
eight days before his body was found. The death of the vagrant
had no apparent connection with a spate of attacks on
homosexuals cruising for sex, and neither Kevin MacDonagh
nor Mark Leyland had been able to put together a good
representation of their assailant's facial characteristics.

Peter Elcock recalls:

> There was nothing going for us. We had put out enquiries
> within the gay community, we had spoken to friends,
> relatives and associates of all the victims we knew about. We
> had appealed through the news media – but nothing came
> back.
>
> By 14 May we were in such a position that the whole future
> of the investigation was looking pretty bleak. The only thing
> we could do was take a bit of a gamble and positively link the
> Connolly and Cole assaults.
>
> It was quite a gamble, on reflection: the two attacks had
> taken place at Vauxhall and at Brixton – so there was no
> match there. David Cole's description of the man who tried to
> kill him couldn't be matched to the man who did murder Tony
> Connolly because there were no witnesses in that case.
>
> The only thing left was Cole's clear recollection of what his
> attacker looked like, and the possibility that the man might
> still be frequenting gay pubs and clubs. We asked Cole if he
> would take us around the circuit to see if he could spot him.

The move was an act of desperation – dangerous and costly.
At 10.15 pm on Thursday, 15 May – two weeks after his ordeal
– David Cole was picked up by two plain-clothes sergeants and
driven to the Prince of Wales pub in Coldharbour Lane,
Brixton. Outside, a back-up unit watched and waited, as the
three men moved through the crowded bars.

I felt terribly nervous. I spent my time observing customers, but I didn't see the man who attacked me. We then went to two more pubs, and I circulated through the bars with the two detectives watching me. But still I could see no sign of the man.

One of the detectives suggested that we return to the Prince of Wales. We reached there at about 12.30 am. I walked around the pub and the dance floor, drinking Perrier water.

I walked to various points in the pub and observed the customers. It was crowded, with people drinking, standing around or dancing. After about twenty minutes I noticed a tall slim man with dark coloured hair. He was standing at the bar with a group of two or three people, having previously walked right past me. I immediately recognised him as the man who had attacked me.

I felt he was unaware of my presence, but my stomach turned over. I wasn't exactly scared, though, because I knew police officers were around me. I went straight over to the other side of the bar and told the detectives I had seen the man who had tried to strangle me.

I went and stood in front of the man – about two or three feet away from him – and said, 'Don't I know you?' He said, 'No – I don't think so. My name is Michele, I'm French and a musician.' He offered me his right hand to shake, which I did because I wanted to get the feel of the man's hands and skin: I know the man who attacked me had soft skin.

His whole manner whilst talking to me was the same as the man who had attacked me – his head was slightly stooped, his manner quiet and his tone softly spoken. I knew I was looking into the eyes of the man who had tried to kill me.

Michele Lupo did not struggle when Detective Sergeants Gary Townsend and Dennis Gregory gripped his arms and propelled him firmly out of the pub into the night air. From Coldharbour Lane it was a short drive to the AMIP HQ at Croydon.

The first thing that struck Peter Elcock as odd about their murder suspect was that he declined their offer of a lawyer to assist him. The second was that he readily admitting murdering Tony Connolly and Damien McClusky.

> He was incredibly calm. He just sat there as we went through
> the allegations with him. Then he said he did the murders.
> The next day we interviewed him again and he admitted the
> Burns murder, biting off his tongue and smearing faeces over
> the body. As if that wasn't enough he told us he had also tried
> to pull the man's eyes out.
>   There was no question of him trying to duck responsibility
> for what he had done. I asked him whether he knew what he
> was doing when he was killing the men and he said he did,
> that he wasn't drunk but he couldn't really think of an
> explanation for the murders.

Peter Elcock asked the questions about Lupo's state of mind
gingerly. The law relating to insanity is quite precise:
defendants are considered legally sane until they prove otherwise, and the test is whether or not they are 'labouring under
such a defect of reason from disease of the mind as not to know
the nature or quality of the act they were doing'.

Alternatively, defendants can plead that whilst they did
know what they were doing they did not – by reason of this
defect of reason – know it was wrong. Once successfully
pleaded, there is only one verdict open to a jury in even the
most serious cases of murder – not guilty by reason of insanity.
(This will not prevent the insane killer being locked up; the
difference is that instead of prison, an indeterminate spell in a
'special hospital', like Broadmoor, will be imposed.)

Michele Lupo availed himself of none of these defences,
which fact, with the inexorable logic of the law, made him
perfectly sane. It was a view with which Peter Elcock had some
difficulty.

> This guy sat there and ultimately admitted four murders and
> three attempted murders. He couldn't give us a clue as to why
> he had done them, other than to say that he felt society had
> abused him and now he was getting his own back. He was
> angry, no doubt about that; but he didn't seem to have any
> idea of what he was angry about.
>   And the killings themselves involved more than your
> average degree of viciousness. I mean, you try explaining to
> the general public why a man would want to do what Lupo did
> – and that he wasn't raving mad.

Although Michele Lupo gave Elcock and Shoemake sufficient evidence to support his unruffled confessions to serial
murder, the detectives felt that they needed to attempt some
explanation of his motive: after all, written and taped confessions have been withdrawn before at the doors of the court, at
which point the traditional trinity of police investigation –
motive, opportunity and circumstantial evidence – have to be
brought into play.

What ensued was a journey into even darker areas of human
sexuality than the AMIP team had embarked on thus far. It
would take them from the heights of fashionable West End
high society to the sordid depths of sado-masochistic rituals in
seedy Earls Court basements. It was a trek that, for some,
would leave an indelible scar.

Michele Lupo had been born in Italy thirty-three years
earlier. His Criminal Records Office entry lists the exact date
as 19 January 1953, but does not specify the town where he
grew up.

He attended the Leonardo Da Vinci secondary school somewhere in 'Northern Italy' until he reached the age of 16.
Between 1969 and 1971 his only known accomplishments were
a correspondence course in languages and a brief study of art.

In 1971, at the age of 18, Lupo was drafted into the
Bersaglieri 22 Commando Unit to complete his two years'
national service. The Italian army does not disclose just what it
imparts to trainee commandos during their period of intensive
military education, but it would be highly unusual if the course
did not include tuition in the variety of techniques recommended for swift and silent killing.

In June 1974 Michele Lupo arrived at Heathrow airport.
Barring occasional forays into the demi-monde of gay clubs in
Amsterdam and Paris, he would remain in London until his
arrest twelve years later.

Initially he began work as a hairdresser in Motcombe Street,
London SW11. It was a job that would last three years: in 1977
Lupo simply disappeared, reappearing only in 1980 and in
somewhat more refined surroundings. For four years, from

March 1980 to March 1984, he worked for the perfume and fashion house Yves St Laurent, beginning as a sales assistant at its headquarters in the Brompton Road, and finishing as manager of the branch.

It was here that Lupo began to cultivate a circle of wealthy socialite friends and acquaintances. The former commando turned hair stylist became, for a time, the darling of the London glitterati. It was a love affair that would ultimately return to haunt them.

Peter Elcock recalls:

> Lupo wasn't exclusively homosexual. We discovered early on
> – in fact he told us – that he quite liked going with women.
> And a lot of women, as well as men, found him attractive.
>   The problem was that he had AIDS. It was left up to us as a
> squad to try and trace as many of his recent lovers as we could
> and advise them to have an HIV test. You can imagine it
> wasn't a particularly pleasant job.
>   Because he had got in with the trendy set we had to break
> the news to a lot of society people – men and women. I
> personally had to ask one very prominent lady socialite
> whether she had slept with Lupo. When she admitted it I had
> to suggest as gently as I could that she should go down to a
> clinic for sexually transmitted diseases.
>   But then I discovered Lupo had also slept with her
> husband, and I had to go round and break the news to him
> about the AIDS without, of course, telling either of them
> about the other's involvement. It was a bloody nightmare.

Not unnaturally, perhaps, Shoemake and Elcock at first advanced the theory that Lupo had started his murderous career as a direct result of anger at contracting AIDS. But that attractively neat possibility was denied by Lupo in one of the several recorded interviews between police and killer – though such denials may conceal more than they reveal.

In it Lupo's only attempt at explaining his actions is to suggest that he felt 'abused' by a number of people over any number of years.

I felt so shitty having been used and abused in the past it was

> just anger . . . I knew what I was doing. I could say I feel sorry
> but I'm not: I had a clear mind, I knew what I was doing. I
> wasn't drunk: I knew – so what's the point of saying sorry?
> I'm not. I don't believe in things unless I've experienced
> them. I've tried drugs but it's not a turn on . . . I enjoy being
> out of my cell, so if you want to go through with it [another
> interview], go through with it: I've nothing more to tell you.

And after that limited self-justification he fell silent.

It was never clear to detectives whether this abuse was experienced at the hands of his fashionable chums, or whether it was a more general dissatisfaction with society at large. But something appears to have caused a rift between Lupo and London's glitterati: in 1984 he ceased to work for Yves St Laurent.

There is no record of why Michele Lupo left the comfortable and privileged surroundings of a renowned fashion house, but from August 1984 he took a series of poorly paid jobs as a shop assistant in boutiques from Earls Court to Oxford Street. At the time of his arrest he was earning the relatively lowly salary of £12,000 a year.

Not that this was his only source of income. It is standard procedure for all police forces that upon arrest a suspect's name should be run through the enormous and powerful database which forms the police national computer. According to Peter Elcock they swiftly discovered that Michele Lupo was no stranger to the law.

> The computer threw up a conviction in that name dating
> back to March 1977. It was for gross indecency – that usually
> means buggery in a public place, and is quite frequently the
> sort of charge brought against homosexual prostitutes. Lupo
> had been fined £40.
> Although the details were sketchy it seemed to fit in with
> some of the things we'd found in his flat. They also suggested
> that he had been operating a prostitution business at some
> point, and that the services he had provided weren't of the
> normal variety.

Michele Lupo had taken out an advert offering the services of

'Rudi', a homosexual masseur. Rudi turned out to be Lupo and the massage no more than an appetiser for the sex which was the real commodity for sale.

But the sex was not conventional by even homosexual standards. Elcock found letters addressed to 'Sir' which pleaded with 'Rudi' to torture the writer with chains, whips, crops, clamps, weights and a device to hang its owner for a lengthy period.

Even the walls of Lupo's flat suggested a man set apart from the rest of the homosexual community: some of its walls were painted jet black and decorated only with the traditional satanic symbols of inverted crosses. But on that subject as on every other possible motive Michele Lupo kept his own counsel.

We came to the conclusion from everything we saw that Lupo was an extremely sadistic type. It took us some time but we eventually discovered what the metal tube found at the scene of Burns's murder had been used for.

There is, apparently, a small but dedicated group of sado-masochistic homosexuals who practise what they call pet shop sex. This involves introducing a small rodent into the passive man's anus via a metal tube. It is clearly incredibly dangerous – not to say cruel – but then the whole business was like that.

We believe that this was one part of Michele Lupo's activities and that some of his victims may have been attracted to this particularly deviant sado-masochistic sex.

You can't imagine the effect on some of the officers on the squad as these enquiries progressed. To be honest I just tried to put the implications and consequences of what we were finding out to the back of my mind – though I never forgot them.

But for some of the lads the effect was terrible. I never found out till much later, long after Lupo was jailed for life, how badly some had taken the case.

I was at a dinner-dance we held every year for the squad and their wives. During the evening one of the wives came up to me and began talking about how oddly her husband had been behaving during the Lupo case.

We were all working very long days – and sometimes nights – on the job. Normally we'd have a drink as a way of winding down. But when this officer got home, generally very late in the evening, he started getting his young kid out of bed, getting him dressed and putting him in the pushchair.

It didn't matter what time it was, he would then take the kid for a walk, a long walk, round the streets. Just him and the baby walking round in the early hours. It turned out that the stuff he was handling in the Lupo investigation had really got to him badly, and the only way he could cope was if he had some sort of normality to return to at the end of the day. For him normality was his kid, taking the baby out for a walk. So he had to do it. It was his way of getting through.

Don't let anyone tell you that this job doesn't have an effect on the officers who do it. And it affects the families too. That's often where the strain shows up worst.

4
The Perfect
Murder

He thought he had done it, got away with
it. He really believed he had committed
the perfect murder.

*Superintendent John Bassett, Croydon,
April 1991*

It is an undeniable, if uncomfortable, truth that the
single most dangerous place for a woman to be is in her own
home. Statistics show that it is within their own four walls that
women are most commonly attacked, raped or killed.

The Home Office crime figures for 1989 make the point
starkly: of the 234 women murdered in England and Wales
that year, 189 – or 81 per cent – died at the hands of husband,
lover, family or close friend. By far the biggest single category
of killer – 41 per cent of all cases – was the husband or
ex-husband.

On Friday, 30 March 1990 the name of Yogannaigaa
Cooppen was added to the new year's growing tally.

The island of Mauritius lies 500 miles off the eastern coast of
Madagascar, and is surrounded by a handful of satellite islands
which together house a population of just over one million.

Discovered originally by Arab navigators in the fourteenth
century, Mauritius has been occupied since then by at least
three colonial powers. First the Dutch, then the French, and

ultimately the British claimed its 1,865 square miles for their
respective empires.

France formally ceded the islands to Britain as part of the
1814 Treaty of Paris, and London ruled the country with a
succession of governors general until Harold Wilson's Labour
government granted independence on 12 March 1968.

Independence, however, entailed remaining within the
Commonwealth. This gave Britain continuing access to the
island's natural resources of sugar, tea, tobacco and hardwood;
in return Mauritian citizens had, for a time at least, the right to
settle in Britain.

It was a benefit enjoyed and taken up by a significant number
of Mauritians who were prepared to sacrifice the rather more
pleasant sub-tropical climate for the prospect of a more
financially rewarding life in Britain.

In 1976 Nadesse and Yogannaigaa Cooppen joined the influx
of those in search of their fortune amid the streets and suburbs
of South London.

Theirs had been an arranged marriage, in the tradition of
Mauritian families. Yogannaigaa, known as Jini, was born in a
small village in September 1957; Nadesse, known as Vijay,
eight years earlier on another part of the island.

In 1973 their respective parents had met to arrange the
match. Shortly after, and before the wedding had taken place,
Jini became pregnant. Almost immediately, and with his
family's blessing, Vijay left for London, taking menial jobs to
earn enough money to support his new family. He worked
variously as a hotel porter and hospital auxiliary first in
Carshalton, Surrey, later at Worthing General Hospital. Here
the duties periodically included wrapping up dead bodies with a
sterile winding sheet in the mortuary.

At the same time he began an affair with a Mauritian
woman living close to the hospital. He concealed, for a time at
least, the existence of the affair from Jini, to whom he would
occasionally write.

In 1976 Vijay had earned enough to return to Mauritius and
claim his wife and young son. It was to be a short stay. On 18

November 1976, the Cooppen family arrived at Heathrow to begin a new life together in the relatively quiet surroundings of Wimbledon.

Almost from the start the marriage began to deteriorate. Vijay was old-fashioned in his approach to a man's rights and responsibilities; Jini had become more modern, more of a liberated westerner than a traditional Mauritian wife. The spectre of Vijay's extra-marital fling came back to haunt the couple, and when her husband persisted in sleeping with the other woman, Jini felt she had the right to protest.

Vijay Cooppen failed to see his wife's point of view. Men and women, he reasoned, were different: a man's sexual needs were his own business and should not provoke wifely complaints when he chose to satisfy them. To emphasise his opinions he beat Jini up. Soon a pattern emerged. Vijay would be unfaithful, Jini complain, and Vijay attack her.

It did not take long for her to decide that the best way to protect herself was to run away. The pattern altered: adultery, reproach, assault, followed by walk out. But Jini never stayed away for long: her upbringing had led her to believe that she should attempt to keep her family together. It was an ingrained tradition boosted by a naive hope that she might somehow find a way to retain her husband's affections.

For more than a year the beatings continued. Finally, late in 1977, she walked out of the house and into the offices of Wimbledon social services. A social worker supplied the address of a refuge for battered women and the name of a good solicitor. The idea was to take legal action against Vijay — divorce, formal separation and injunctions preventing him from approaching her were the major options outlined. Criminal proceedings for assault were not ruled out.

But the plan came to nothing. A summons was issued for her husband to attend the county court, but records unearthed by Superintendent John Bassett thirteen years later show that no action was taken against Vijay Cooppen.

We should not be unduly surprised. Wife battering was – and to a large extent remains – an ill-understood and unaddressed problem. When it was discussed, it was all too frequently as a man's right, joke or a sexual stimulant. The fact that women were being beaten, bruised, maimed and killed seemed somehow to be forgotten.

The legal right of men to 'chastise' their wives as often as they saw fit had existed until 1862. The sole restriction on this historic liberty was on the size of the stick they used to beat women into submission: legitimate weapons, the courts held, were to be no thicker than a man's thumb.

Although this barbaric law of male supremacy had been ended, its legacy remained. The response of statutory agencies to allegations of domestic violence remained uncomprehending and unhelpful and rape within marriage would not be deemed illegal until 1991.

The first woman's refuge had been set up in 1971. Erin Pizzey was then running a playgroup in South London. One day a young mother appeared: she bore the bruises of a vicious and sustained attack, and was quite literally shaking with fear at the prospect of meeting her assailant again. She knew her attacker well: she was married to, and lived with, him.

Pizzey took her in and gave her sanctuary. It was the beginning of the refuge movement: Chiswick Women's Aid (later re-named Chiswick Family Rescue) was the first safe house anywhere in the world for victims of domestic violence. From then on it was a constant struggle to find funding to provide sufficient shelters for the number of women coming forward and seeking sanctuary.

Erin Pizzey mobilised support by taking the campaign to the media. As the women's movement grew so did newspaper and television coverage of horror stories emerging from the refuges. But the publicity changed little. A relative handful of men may have altered their attitude to a woman's right to live free from brutality, but the annual crime statistics proved that increasing numbers of women were recorded as victims of violence ranging from common assault, through grievous bodily harm to murder.

It took another four years for the first formal response to

emerge. In 1975 a parliamentary select committee held a series
of hearings into domestic violence. It studied the available data
for several months before announcing: 'Despite our efforts we
are unable to give any estimates of what the likely numbers [of
women abused by their husbands or lovers] are . . . We were
hampered by the remarkable paucity of information about
domestic violence.'

One of the reasons for that dearth of knowledge was that,
whatever the letter of the law, most police forces treated a
man's assault on his wife in the home as far less serious than a
comparable attack on a stranger in the street. The 1990 Home
Office Circular No. 60 highlighted this dichotomy: 'In the past
police officers arriving at the scene of domestic violence have
often tried to smooth over the dispute and reconcile the
partners. Research shows that this is not necessarily the best
course of action.'

As ever, the Home Office was expressing diplomatically the
true nature of traditional police attitudes to abuse of women.
Incidents of wife-beating were referred to – and frequently still
are – as 'fish and chip' disputes, as if the cosy imagery of a
traditional English tea-time could somehow explain or excuse
the shattered bones and black eyes which were their
frequent consequences.

Many such instances were routinely 'no crimed' by investigating officers – an administrative convenience by which they
were freed from proceeding against a violent man. The basis for
these decisions was typically either that the abuser apologised
and appeared contrite, or that the woman was too scared to say
in front of her tormentor that she wanted him to be charged.
There is a painful inevitability to what must often have
happened when the officers left.

The select committee report also noted that there were too
few refuges to meet the demands from abused women. It
recommended that at least 800 shelters were needed just to
give victims of domestic violence a brief stay in some form of
safe house. Like much else before and after it, the call went
unheeded.

Jini Cooppen found that the only way to escape her husband's continuing brutality was to return to Mauritius. In 1980 she and the couple's 5-year-old son, Nagaissen, sought refuge with her parents and stayed for four months. The end came after Vijay's mother pressurised Jini to return to London and give the marriage another chance. To make sure there were no last-minute hiccups, she accompanied her daughter-in-law and grandson on the return journey.

For a time Vijay appeared genuinely to have mended his ways. Family life in their house in Flemming Mead, Wimbledon, was as happy as Jini had ever known. But when his mother flew back to Mauritius, Vijay reverted to type: the beatings began again.

It is a testament to Jini's courage and strength of purpose that she managed to survive. As 1981 progressed in a familiar pattern of violence, she set about organising legal restraints upon her violent husband. In January 1982 she obtained a formal separation order and with it custody of Nagaissen and the right to stay in their home. Vijay was unceremoniously evicted.

It was not a verdict he found able to accept. The very notion of his wife demanding and being granted an order against him was irreconcilable with his upbringing and beliefs. So great was his anger that Jini began to fear for her life.

Monday, 14 March 1983 saw the culmination of years of maltreatment. Jini was at home with Nagaissen when Vijay came to the house. He was legally barred from entering what had been the couple's home, but he did so nonetheless. He chased his estranged wife upstairs; to escape him she jumped from a window on the first floor.

It is possible to survive such falls with only cuts and bruises – possible but not common. Jini Cooppen fell heavily, injuring her back. As she lay in hospital in the days and weeks afterwards, she had only one immediate consolation: Vijay was charged with causing her grievous bodily harm.

It took several months for her injuries to heal fully, and nearly nine months before Vijay appeared at Croydon Crown

Court to face his accuser. The result was a twelve-month sentence and an eventual £130,000 award from the Criminal Injuries Compensation Board – the official state body which measures injuries caused by criminal behaviour and matches them to a sliding scale of ex-gratia payments.

The windfall gave Jini Cooppen her first taste of financial freedom. She quickly filed for, and was granted, a divorce, and with Nagaissen moved across town to North Road, Wimbledon.

If nothing else, Vijay Cooppen was persistent. On his release from prison he began paying court once again to the woman he had very nearly killed. He must also have been persuasive: late in 1986 he and Jini were reconciled and began to share a bed in the home she had acquired with the money 'bought' with her back injury. A year later she gave birth to a daughter.

By 1987 when Vijay once again began beating his wife, the Metropolitan Police had begun to undergo a change. The then Commissioner, Sir Kenneth Newman, had set up a working party to examine domestic violence and his Force's response to it; in 1986 it reported, and the following year a number of initiatives were set in motion.

There is a bitter irony in the report. Newman had been, prompted to commission it after seeing a comprehensive Canadian study on the aims and operations of specialised domestic violence units within individual police districts. Chief among the Canadian conclusions were that wife-beating was no less a crime than assaulting a perfect stranger and that the pattern of evidence showed that attacks increased rather than diminished if left untackled. This was precisely the point made – and ignored – by the parliamentary select committee eleven years before.

Newman's response was to issue a Force Directive that required for the first time incidents of domestic violence to be recorded as serious crimes. Experimental domestic violence units were set up where plain clothes officers, mostly women, listened sympathetically, and organised active intervention in what had previously been an unofficial no-go area. According to WPC Lynn Robinson, who joined the Streatham DVU after thirteen years in the Met., 'In the old days nothing much would be done – you would go out on a [domestic] call, tell them to quieten down and that would be that. Husband/wife rows were taboo: it was down to them.'

When, in 1987, Jini decided again to seek police help not all police districts within London had DVUs.† For once she was lucky: Wimbledon was the site of one of the early units, and she was greeted sympathetically. Social workers, too, offered support and advice, but for reasons of her own Jini Cooppen decided against a second separation and divorce.

The reason was partly to be found in the rough and ready arrangement the couple had come to by themselves. Vijay now slept alone on the settee in the lounge, and his wife was exerting both social and financial independence.

Provoked beyond endurance by her husband's perpetual meanness with money to support the family, she had found a job as an agency nurse with a local company called Care Alternatives. The wages she earnt from shifts at hospitals and old people's homes, added to the remaining money from her Criminal Injuries Compensation Board pay-out, had given her a life outside the claustrophobic and frequently violent atmosphere at home. She had her own friends, her own money, and was building a small nest-egg from buying and letting property.

Vijay, too, had rather more lucrative employment, working as a postman at the New Malden sorting office, a short drive away from the house in North Road. A new Volvo sat in the drive testifying to the improved wages and the success of his own speculation on the property markets in South London and Mauritius.

But his wife's western-style freedom irked and rankled. He

† It was to take until 1991 for an almost complete network of forty-three such units to be established within the Metropolitan Police. Despite Home Office instructions, outside London only two regional forces – West Yorkshire and Northumbria – had similar schemes.

wanted – he needed – to control what she did and who she saw.
According to Superintendent John Bassett:

> Jini used to complain bitterly about her husband's meanness
> with money, and the fact that he constantly opened her mail,
> listened to her telephone conversations and generally gave
> her no privacy whatsoever.
>   To thwart his snooping into what she saw as her affairs she
> kept all her private papers together in her handbag: family
> allowance books, building society account books, letters to
> mortgage brokers and solicitors about her property
> transactions – they were all kept safe in her bag. And she
> carried that bag with her absolutely everywhere.

In one thing alone – aside from his own needs – Vijay was
generous. Their son, Nagaissen, was sent to an expensive local
private school. Vijay was happy enough to pay out the £800 it
cost per term – Nagaissen, after all, was a boy and a boy would
become a man. His daughter, however, received no such special
treatment. She attended the council's special free nursery for
'socially deprived children'.

Life for Jini Cooppen became ever more difficult. To circum-
vent her husband's obsessive interference in her affairs she set
up a series of accommodation addresses – commercial mail-
holding boxes – in false names. Care Alternatives sent her
wage cheques to these addresses, frequently made out to
'Jenny Cooppen' or 'Jenny Curten'.

In December 1989 her brother Reuben turned up at the
house in North Road. He asked Jini for help to buy a small flat
on the other side of Wimbledon. She agreed, with the proviso
that if ever Vijay's attacks became more than she could bear,
Reuben would allow her to use the flat as a sanctuary.

Most of Jini's capital had been invested in property of her
own. The only way to raise enough money quickly was to
re-mortgage 17 North Road. She knew that Vijay would be less
than pleased, but reasoned that it was her house not his, and
that she could keep the arrangement secret from him. She
failed to take into account her husband's obsessive snooping.

Between January and March 1990 Jini carefully made

arrangements to raise £30,000 on the re-mortgage. She consulted a firm of high street solicitors in Mitcham, Surrey, a twenty-minute car drive from her home. Ultimately she agreed on a contract with the Northern Rock Building Society.

To get the best financial benefit from the transaction, the remortgage needed to be complete and authorised by 30 March at the latest. Jini impressed upon her solicitors how vital the deadline had become, and they laboured to meet it.

On Tuesday, 27 March the building society notified her by letter that a cheque for £30,000 had been placed with her solicitors. That letter was to prove quite literally fatal. Vijay intercepted it and, as usual, read it without invitation. Immediately he set about obstructing the remortgage.

Two days later, on Thursday, 29 March, Jini's solicitors received an urgent call from a clerk at the Land Registry, the government department which records and formalises the ownership of all land and buildings throughout Britain.

There appeared to be a problem with the re-mortgage of 17 North Road: the Charge Register was now showing a Notice of Occupation in favour of Vijay Cooppen. The solicitors sent a hurried letter to Jini by motorcycle courier, explaining that her husband's claim to occupation rights in the house was effectively blocking the completion of the re-mortgage.

Jini was hysterical with anger and frustration. Vijay's interference had gone too far this time. She ignored the solicitor's suggestion that the couple should both turn up at his office in Mitcham the next day to sort the disagreement out amicably. Instead she planned to deal with Vijay herself.

She was waiting for him when he got back from the sorting office. She showed him the solicitor's letter, confronting him with the evidence of his meddling. He, in turn, forcefully expressed his views on her financial acumen, the loan to her brother and a woman's duty to her husband.

That Friday Jini was due to work through the night as an agency nurse at a local nursing home for the elderly. Vijay drove her to Rosemary Lodge in The Drive, Wimbledon, at

8.30 pm. They rowed throughout the short journey. According to Vijay he never saw his wife again.

The daily routine at 17 North Road usually started with the Cooppens' lodger – a labourer by name of Carl Smith – leaving the house at 6.00 am. When Jini was on night duty, Vijay would wake the children and get them breakfast. Jini would catch a bus from work and arrive home around 8.30, just in time to accompany her husband and daughter on the drive to nursery. Vijay would then drop his wife off at home and proceed on to the sorting office.

On Friday, 30 March, the family's routine was altered forever. Vijay would later claim that Jini never came home and that, worried and frustrated, he telephoned Rosemary Lodge only to be told that she had left there some time before. According to Superintendent John Bassett:

> His story was that she didn't turn up, and he was left with his daughter as time ticked away. He said he was worried about being late for work, and in the end rang a friend, asking her to look after the little girl until Jini arrived home.
>
> He then went to work and – except for a forty-minute lunchtime trip to Rosemary Lodge to ascertain whether there was any reason for his wife's disappearance – was there all day. He added that he got home around 7.00 pm to find his son in his room but no sign of Jini.
>
> As a result he drove round to his friend, collected his daughter and then telephoned a number of Jini's friends to see if she was with them.
>
> When he failed to find her that way he phoned up Wimbledon police station and finally, at 11.30 pm, turned up at the front desk to report his wife as being missing.

Missing persons enquiries are depressingly common: in large urban communities it is rare that a week goes by without a distressed husband, wife or parent walking in off the street to report the disappearance of a relative.

But since there is, as yet, no national register of such reports, much less a computer database which could link them with alleged sightings, police and hospital accident data or descriptions of unidentified bodies, there is little the average local station can do.

Standard police procedure is to take the details, circulate them as and where possible within a relatively small local network and notify the Metropolitan Police Missing Persons Bureau at New Scotland Yard. Wider enquiries are typically left to the network of voluntary groups – many of them Christian – who attempt to coordinate the chaos of disintegrating families, runaway children and people seeking sanctuary at hostels for the homeless or abused women's shelters. It is far from an exact science.

The disappearance of Yogannaigaa 'Jini' Cooppen might have languished as just another case in already over-stuffed files had it not been for Leslie Farren.

At 5.00 am on Saturday, 31 March, Leslie Farren was setting up his market stall in front of Arch 535 in Orphanage Yard, Brixton. The small alley-way runs alongside British Rail's South-Eastern network main line. Traders and entrepreneurial small businessmen regularly hawk their wares along its 75 yards of archways.

Farren was being helped that morning by three teenage boys whose job was to open up the arch doors and help set out stalls along the alley. As it grew light he saw a body lying across the front of Arch 535.

By 5.15 am local beat constables reported the body as that of an Asian woman, between 30 and 35 years old, dressed in a beige raincoat, black skirt and black and white jumper. All the clothing appeared to have ridden – or been dragged – up. There were no tights or stockings on the body and – more remarkably for a damp March morning – no shoes. Within an hour a police surgeon had pronounced the woman dead.

John Bassett was summoned from his bed and arrived at Orphanage Yard at 8.00 am, with a pathologist, forensic science officer, and his own 'bagman' sergeant in tow. It was clear from the outset that this was likely to be a murder enquiry, and one requiring the skills of the AMIP. This view was based on a swift observation of the area around the corpse.

There was no sign of a struggle – which indicated that the woman had been killed elsewhere and then dumped in front of the arch. Equally, and unusually, the body had been stripped of jewellery, shoes and any form of identification. Individually, any one of those three factors could have pointed to an element of organisation in the killing: taken together it told Bassett that whoever murdered the woman had taken a good deal of trouble to delay her identification.

An initial examination suggested that she had been strangled anything up to twenty-four hours earlier. There were no signs of sexual assault, which ruled out rape as the motive; if she had been robbed there was a puzzling lack of bruising or defensive wounds. When the divisional photographer had recorded the scene from countless angles and perspectives Bassett gave permission for the body to be moved. The next time he would see it would be on a slab at Greenwich Mortuary.

The removal of a body from the place where it is found follows an invariable pattern. First, the victim's hands and feet are seal-wrapped in plastic bags: the aim is to safeguard any minute fragments that adhere to their surface or are caught underneath the nails. Frequently victims scratch at their attacker's face, and their frenetic clawing drags skin or hair from the murderer. Although microscopic these can be enough for forensic scientists to analyse to the point where they can match resulting data with similar samples from the suspect.

Next the doctor or police surgeon presses a thermometer into the rectum of the corpse. The purpose of this seemingly macabre ritual is to record the body temperature at the time of discovery. An additional reading is made noting the ambient temperature in the area around the victim. In turn these will be compared with subsequent tests to determine the likely time of death.

Pathologists use a complicated formula to work out an approximate estimate of the number of hours, days or weeks which have passed since the victim died: rectal temperature is an integral part of the calculation.

The human body has a normal living temperature of 37 degrees centigrade. By subtracting the rectal temperature and dividing the result by 1.5, pathologists arrive at a figure which can be compared to the known fact that after eighteen to twenty-four hours, the temperature of a corpse will be the same as the ambient temperature around it. By taking regular rectal temperature readings over a given period he can ultimately deduce the time at which the body last had a 37 degrees temperature – and therefore, the time of death.

If all this seems a somewhat crude and haphazard science as the end of the twentieth century nears, we need to remember that it is less than a hundred years since the first reliable test to differentiate human from animal blood was established.

For all the advances in forensic science made in the second half of this century – discoveries we shall consider in Chapter Five – there remains something faintly primitive about even the most modern post-mortem examination. Almost the sole concession to modern technology will be the small micro-cassette recorder into which the examiner dictates his actions and findings.

After beginning his series of rectal tests, the pathologist starts his autopsy by simply looking at the corpse. Evidence of decomposition is first on the list: not merely do dead bodies conform to a relatively precise timescale of decay – variable only by factors of surrounding temperature and the amount of clothing left on them – but an entire cast of minute insects and organisms may invade the cadaver.

The study of the habits and life-cycle of these creatures can provide vital information as to the length of time the corpse has lain undisturbed. Forensic entomology is frequently seen as a new breakthrough in the science of pathology – police forces are increasingly calling in academic experts on Phorid or 'coffin' flies and the mating habits of bluebottles – but its origins date back at least fifty years.

Professor Cedric Keith Simpson of Guy's Medical School became, during the Second World War, the most widely consulted of all forensic scientists. It was his pioneering study of the breeding cycle of bluebottle maggots, on behalf of police investigating the discovery of a rotting corpse, that first took the scientific detection of murder into new and revealing territory.

Lividity is the second simple eye-test carried out at the post-mortem. Blood is kept pumping round the human body by the heart: once the heart stops, blood invariably obeys the law of gravity and drains down to the lowest part of the body. Or almost invariably: moving a body after death can temporarily interrupt the process, and delay the appearance of the tell-tale signs of large amounts of blood collecting under the skin.

Rigor mortis is an additional indicator of the time of death: a dead body begins to stiffen within five hours of life being extinguished, starting with the eye-lids, moving to the lower jaw and thence downwards to the shoulders, arms, trunk and legs. At twelve hours after death, *rigor* is fully established: at twenty-four hours it begins to disappear and at thirty-six hours is gone completely. Nor can the symptom reappear. The stiffness is caused by muscle protein coagulating and producing a temporary shortening of the muscle itself.

But *rigor mortis*, like rectal temperature calculations, is an imprecise science: it is affected by ambient temperature, layers of fat (thin people cool more quickly than those better padded), and the quantity of clothing worn at the moment of death. It gives nothing more than a good 'guesstimate' of the time life expired.

Rather more accurate assessments can be made from the state of the fluid around the eyes which dries on an established and less variable sliding scale. Equally, a careful examination of the body for any obvious wounds can tell the pathologist whether these were inflicted before or after death – the latter being crucial both in pin-pointing possible aberrant behaviour indicative of a Disorganised serial murderer, and in assessing the truth of any subsequent statements made by the suspected killer.

If the wounds were made before death there will be visible evidence of inflammation around the injury: small 'doctor' cells in the human body called leukocytes are known to arrive at the wound in a precise sequence over a 48-hour period. Measuring the number of such cells – or indeed their absence – can tell the pathologist whether the injury pre- or post-dated the death.

Once this visual inspection is complete, and the resultant information recorded on micro-cassette, the first incision will be made. Modern pathologists open bodies to a set pattern – a Y-shaped cut starting under both nipples and continuing in a straight line down to the pubis. All vital organs are then removed and individually preserved.

If the post-mortem technique is relatively inefficient in pinning down a precise time a murder occurred, its major strength lies in establishing the exact cause of death.

The autopsy examination of Jini Cooppen disclosed that she had indeed been asphyxiated, and that her killer had stood behind her compressing her windpipe by tightening his arm against her throat. A mark on her shoulder suggested she had, at some point after death, been dragged along by her feet. There was, additionally, a curious lack of dirt or dust on the body – unusual given the dirty arch where it had been found: John Bassett rapidly came to the conclusion that Jini had been killed somewhere fairly clean early on the morning of Friday, 30 March, wrapped in something like a sheet, and then dumped in the alley in Brixton some hours later.

As a matter of routine he ordered a check to be made with the Missing Persons Bureau at New Scotland Yard: any reports of the disappearance of a young Asian woman in the previous twenty-four hours were to be sent up to the AMIP HQ in Croydon. It took only a few minutes for the Bureau to dig out the details of Vijay Cooppen's appearance at Wimbledon police station the previous night.

Whilst the pathologist carried out his detailed examination of the remains of Jini Cooppen, the Metropolitan Police Forensic Science Laboratory at Lambeth was examining the clothing in which she had been found and a tyre mark discovered some yards away in the alley.

The first police forensic science laboratory in Britain was established not in London but Nottingham. Captain Athelstan Popkess, Chief Constable of Nottinghamshire Constabulary, set up a joint operation with the city's University College. By 1931 the small but efficient unit was fully operational, and had been copied by police in Sheffield and Cardiff. The Metropolitan Police had to wait another three years before the first dedicated forensic science laboratory came on stream: the delay was inevitably caused by political wrangling over the cost. Neither the Home Office nor the senior police management wanted to pick up the bill for what would be an extremely well-equipped service.

The pressure to create not just the London service but a network of seven regional units was increased by the return to Britain of the former chief government chemist of Ceylon, one C. T. Symons. He made himself available to the Home Office as an advisor: his recommendations were hard to ignore, and in 1934 the first Metropolitan Police Forensic Laboratory opened for business in the North London suburb of Hendon. It was an overnight success, yielding vital evidence which helped convict a string of killers.

By the time Jini Cooppen's clothing turned up for examination in sealed plastic sacks, the laboratory had both earnt a formidable reputation as an integral part of routine police investigations into all serious crime, and was suffering the first repercussions of the laxity and over-enthusiasm with which some of its past scientists had approached major terrorist cases.

First the Guildford Four, then the Birmingham Six and finally the Maguire Seven: dubious or distorted forensic evidence had played a part in their convictions and in a remarkable twelve-month period was the cause of their ultimate release.

The tests on Jini Cooppen's clothing were in a different league from those applied in search of evidence of bombmaking materials. There was a lot less of it, for a start – just a partial footprint discernible on her beige raincoat – and it would require a simple process of matching rather than any complicated chemical analysis to determine whether the pattern matched that of shoes belonging to whoever was ultimately arrested.

The tyre print, too, required straightforward visual examination and eventual comparison. The clear implication was that forensic science could not solve the mystery of Jini Cooppen's murder, only provide corroborative evidence against the killer when police identified him.

That process of identification had already begun. As the pathologist began his post-mortem two detectives called on Vijay asking for a photograph of his missing wife; neither told him they wanted to compare the picture with the body on the mortuary slab, but both noticed something odd about the man's behaviour. They took the photographs back to John Bassett.

> It was obvious that the body and the woman reported missing from home were one and the same: that was our first step accomplished. We had identified the victim. But when they reported to me the officers who had spoken to me both said they found his overall attitude and manner totally inconsistent with the behaviour they would have expected from a man worried about the disappearance of his wife. He appeared to be utterly unmoved by the whole incident, and he had an aversion to looking at them when questioned.
>
> With his permission they looked around the house and in the family car to see if there was any correspondence to indicate where she might be or the reason for her disappearance. They could find nothing.

Later the same day two more detectives returned to the four-bedroomed terraced house at 17 North Road and took formal statements from Vijay and Nagaissen about Jini's disappearance.

Vijay Cooppen told the AMIP team that he had not seen his wife since dropping her off for work at Rosemary Lodge on the Thursday evening. She had not returned the next morning and he had first driven his son to the railway station in time for the

8.00 am train to school, then arranged for his daughter to stay with a friend while he went to work.

Nagaissen corroborated his father's account: he had last seen his mother being driven to work on Thursday night by Vijay; she certainly was not home by the time he left the next morning – though this was not necessarily unusual: Jini's working hours frequently meant that she would not see her son before he left for school.

As the first day of the murder squad's enquiry into Jini Cooppen's death drew to a close, it was already clear to John Bassett that his most likely suspect would be her husband. Not only was that statistically the most probable explanation, but Vijay himself was acting strangely.

Sunday, 1 April 1990 was day two of the investigation. At this stage in an AMIP murder enquiry the pressure begins to build inexorably. No SIO, particularly not one as experienced as Bassett, wants to allow the case to drag on any longer without a clear and winning line of enquiry: seventy-two hours is the informal cut-off point, when the team knows it has a 'sticker' on its hands.

Bassett sent the detectives back to 17 North Road to re-interview Vijay and Nagaissen, and to make another search of the house and car for anything revealing. At the same time other officers were dispatched to track down the night-sister on duty at Rosemary Lodge on Jini's last night there.

Bridget Harling had been the senior nurse at the home on Thursday, 29 March. She told Bassett's men that she had watched Jini leave with two other nurses at 7.30 on the Friday morning.

Mary Kakande and Sharon Khumalo worked for the same agency as Jini Cooppen: Bassett immediately set about tracing them. When he did, their information was revealing.

That night was the first time Sharon Khumalo had worked with Jini Cooppen. The women were drawn to one another quickly and discovered they shared similar marital problems. At around 1.00 am in the middle of their shift, they had a lengthy heart to heart talk and swapped addresses. Jini noted the information down in her diary.

She had been expected to make her way home on public transport, but that morning Mary Kakande had offered both her colleagues a lift in her car. First she dropped Sharon off at her home, then drove round to the corner of Haydons Road and North Road, just a few yards from Number 17. By the end of Mary Kakande's statement it was clear that Jini Cooppen had arrived at her door at 7.50 am.

At the same time that AMIP officers were taking statements from the agency nurses, their colleagues were re-searching the Cooppen family home. In a cupboard by the hall telephone they found Jini's diary and, after logging the fact, carefully placed it in their car for later examination. Next they turned their attention to Vijay's Volvo and recovered Jini's building society account book from the glovebox.

It is standard procedure on murder enquiries for the SIO to arrange an office meeting at least once a day. Almost nothing is allowed to disrupt the gathering at which every officer involved in the case is first asked to summarise the results of his particular line of enquiry, then encouraged to chip in opinions, estimates and hunches for his superior's consideration. John Bassett considers the office meeting the single most valuable part of the investigative routine.

> Absolutely anything goes at them. It's an opportunity for the lads on the ground to push their ideas and information at the SIO completely freely, and it regularly throws up the key to the mystery.
>
> As the senior officer you've got to tread a fine balance between encouraging all these young detectives, and not wasting too much time, but you shouldn't ignore what they have to say. If you do, they'll lose confidence and the will to get this thing solved; equally you may miss the vital line of enquiry.
>
> When I was younger than I am now, I sat in an office meeting on a murder enquiry and the officer in charge just wouldn't listen to what I and some colleagues were saying.
>
> It was clear to us that the murder we were investigating

involved the victim's brother. We kept on about this meeting after meeting, but the SIO wouldn't take it up.

Eventually we were proved right: some other line pointed up the brother's involvement and he was arrested and eventually convicted. But a lot of time could have been saved if the boss had listened to what his officers were saying at the office meeting. It's a lesson I generally try to remember when some young detective is banging on about something at a meeting I'm in charge of.

The office meeting on Sunday, 1 April duly noted the unusual fact of Jini Cooppen's building society book being in her husband's car. Bassett and his team knew by that stage how closely she had guarded all her financial documents against her husband's prying eyes. And then there was the question of time: Vijay had told them that Jini had not returned home by the time he left first to take Nagaissen to the train, and then again at 8.30 am when he left for work, taking their daughter to a friend en route. Yet Mary Kakande had said she dropped Jini off just a few yards from her door at 7.50 am.

Already there was clear suspicion in Bassett's mind that Vijay Cooppen might know a good deal more about his wife's disappearance than he had acknowledged to date. It was an impression strengthened considerably the following day.

On the Monday morning we approached the manager of Care Alternatives, Angela Byrne. She told us about the sometimes complicated arrangements Jini Cooppen made for receiving payment for her nursing shifts.

The normal procedure would be for Mrs Cooppen to submit an invoice for the hours worked – there were fourteen previous ones in the files. On each one there was no signature on the bottom, just the name of Jenny Curten or Jenny Cooppen at the top.

But as the officers talked to Mrs Byrne it became clear that she had just received another invoice, this one being for the night of 29/30 March.

There were two things odd about this invoice. The first was that although it had the name Jenny Curten at the top, there was a signature – 'Y. Cooppen' – at the bottom, which was in different handwriting from the rest of the invoice.

The second puzzle was concerning the delivery of the invoice itself. Care Alternatives is part of an office complex with a letter box round the corner from the entrance. There were seventy envelopes opened that Monday morning but only two had been delivered by hand. One was a white envelope and the officers were able to eliminate that; the other was a small brown one.

We were able to show not just that the envelope had contained the invoice, but, from the evidence of staff working over the weekend, that it had been delivered to Care Alternatives between 1.30 pm on Saturday, 31 March and 4.00 pm the following day.

According to the pathologist Jini Cooppen had been murdered between 8.00 am and 9.00 am on Friday, 30 March – just over an hour at most after Mary Kakande dropped her at the corner of Haydons Road and North Road, and between twenty-four and forty-eight hours before the brown envelope containing the invoice was dropped into Care Alternative's letter box in Worple Road.

Whoever had killed her wanted us to think she had died in the alley-way in Brixton. But what sort of murderer would then take an envelope from her bag and then travel several miles across town to Wimbledon to deliver it by hand?

By Tuesday, 3 April the psychological 72-hour target had passed: Bassett knew that unless he was close to solving the case, the investigation of Jini Cooppen's murder might drag on for several more inconclusive months. Although he harboured deep suspicions about Vijay's story, he needed a good deal more circumstantial evidence to support his theory. It began arriving that morning.

First, the fingerprint branch delivered their verdict on the brown envelope which had been used to deliver the mystery invoice: it bore one recognisable print – that of Vijay Cooppen. It was significant, but not yet conclusive: there could have been any number of innocent explanations for the presence of his prints on what appeared to be his wife's private correspondence.

Next, a search of Vijay's locker at the New Malden sorting office unearthed a letter from the Northern Rock Building Society, addressed to Jini, and a blank invoice from Care Alternatives. Given the detectives' knowledge of the extent to which Jini would go to protect her financial affairs from Vijay's inspection, his claim that she had given him the letter to read seemed unlikely, and his explanation for its presence in the locker did not ring true.

> He said his wife showed him the letter in the kitchen at home and then he took it to work with him. When we asked how it had ended up in the locker not in his pocket, he said he must have taken it out when he changed into his working clothes. But checks with other staff members proved that he never changed his clothes at work because there was no need to. Clearly he was lying, and there was something significant about the letter.
>
> I began to feel confident that what had really happened on the morning of Friday, 30 March centred around the building society re-mortgage.
>
> It seemed highly likely that, having rowed the previous evening about his interference, Jini arrived home to a deserted house about 8.00 am. Vijay would have been taking their son to the train. When he and the little girl got back, the argument flared up again, during which he killed her.

Vijay Cooppen's behaviour had seemed unusual since the night he reported his wife missing. Not only had he been unable to look the desk constable in the eye while compiling the missing persons report, but he had asked two curious questions: how far would the police search for someone who had disappeared, and would they make use of dogs?

John Bassett came to the conclusion that the questions formed part of a carefully executed plan.

> We believe that he had not yet disposed of the body at this point – that is, at 11.30 on the Friday night, more than twelve hours after she died, Jini Cooppen was still lying in the house in North Road. The questions Vijay asked were designed to help him hide the body and disguise the time of disposal so that he could build up an alibi.

Statements taken from passers-by had allowed Bassett to narrow down the time when the body was dumped in Orphanage Yard to between 8.30 pm on Friday and 5.00 am on Saturday. Vijay had alibis for all of that time. Specifically, Nagaissen had told the detectives that his father had been at home with him between midnight and 5.00 am on the morning his mother's body had been discovered.

There was little the AMIP team could do about the alibis until they formed a clearer picture of how Jini's body had been concealed from her children.

We believed that Vijay had killed his wife with their daughter still in the house. But he had obviously not been able to dispose of the corpse with her there. So I decided to test the time it would have taken him to drive the little girl to his friend's house, then drive back home, conceal the body, and then drive on to work in New Malden. The tests showed quite clearly that he would have been able to do all this and still arrive at work at 10.12 am as we knew he had.

The problem we faced was that there was nothing in the house that indicated the method of disposal. We decided there were three possibilities. The first was that he could have had an accomplice – but we never found any evidence to support that theory. It was more likely that he either left the body lying under the bedcover and locked the bedroom door, or that he wrapped the body in a sheet and put it immediately in the boot of his car.

We knew he had worked in a hospital, and that as part of his duties he had wrapped bodies in the mortuary, so that seemed a good line of enquiry. The bed linen, therefore, was going to be important. It was then we discovered that Vijay had washed all the sheets on the evening of Saturday, 31 March.

We checked with our laboratory colleagues who informed us that modern washing powders not only wash whiter than white, they also wash away all forensic evidence, making the sheets useless for examination.

If Vijay's actions had foiled the forensic scientists, they had added to his already suspicious pattern of behaviour. What normal man, Bassett reasoned, washes all the family bed linen less than twelve hours after his wife's body has been found in an alley?

A week after the death of Jini Cooppen a service of mourning was held at 17 North Road. The event was part of Mauritian custom and Vijay seemed anxious to portray himself as the expatriate community would expect a grieving husband to behave. He wore his socks inside out in keeping with the Mauritian folk-tradition that such sartorial inversion wards off evil spirits.

But at times the mask dropped. Vijay's knowledge of tradition was either patchy or slipping when he told friends and detectives alike that he had given Jini £125 as he drove her to work on the last Thursday night of her life.

This broke with the Mauritian custom that money should never be given after 6.00 pm. It also seemed distinctly out of character for a man with a well-earned reputation for meanness. Bassett grew more suspicious still.

> The money was not found on the body of Mrs Cooppen in the alleyway. So either she had been robbed – and that was the impression I believe we were meant to form – or it had never existed except as a ploy to put us on the wrong track.
> There were other things that Cooppen said or did at the mourning service which made it seem more likely that he had some involvement with his wife's death. Some of them seemed to establish a pattern in his behaviour.

There were forty guests at the service, and – quite naturally – some gossiped amongst themselves about the circumstances in which Jini Cooppen had been found. Simla Sonahee was talking quietly with a group of friends after prayers had been said. 'I wonder,' she asked, 'why they took her shoes off?'

Vijay overheard the remark and seemed keen to explain: 'So they don't have any trace.' He seemed curiously forthcoming, so Mrs Sonahee pressed on. 'How could they have taken her shoes off so easily? They must have been laced up because they were nursing shoes.'

Again Vijay had an answer: 'No,' he said, pointing down at

his own feet, 'they were slip-on shoes like mine.' The persistent Mrs Sonahee then raised the question of Jini's missing spectacles. 'Maybe,' Vijay suggested, 'when they were putting the body in the boot they fell off.'

It was a classic slip, worthy of pulp detective fiction: no one had yet suggested to Vijay that his wife might not have died in the Brixton alley, much less that police suspected she had been taken there in the boot of his car.

Later the same evening he appeared, almost for the first time, to be showing the strain his friends expected of a grieving widower. Eshan Tegally suggested a common remedy. 'You look very sad,' he said. 'You should take a few drinks before you go to bed, which will help you keep cool and calm.'

Vijay reacted strongly: 'Absolutely not, no drink. Any time the police can come and question me and I might say something else to what I have already said to them. Then they will come back to me again.'

This dread of police attention matched a statement made a day or so before by another family friend, Sooriah Appaddoo. She had called at 17 North Road to see how he was coping, and was surprised at the tenor of Vijay's conversation.

> The police are going to question you, and you must be careful what you say. I know that you know a lot that goes on in this house, and you haven't heard my side of the story. Whatever you say it won't bring Jini back. They might accuse me wrongly and send me to prison, and the children will suffer.

Vijay Cooppen's fears were well-founded. John Bassett had decided on his line of enquiry and it centred around checking and double-checking every last detail of Vijay's statements, movements and alibis.

In part this had been caused by the discovery on the Police National Computer of his previous conviction for causing grievous bodily harm to Jini.

The circumstances set out in the file which Bassett drew from the Metropolitan Police central registry added to his view of Vijay Cooppen as a man capable of planning and executing a careful cover-up of his actions.

> One of the bits of evidence which had led to his conviction for GBH centred around footwear. It seemed to me that this could be a reason for the disappearance of Mrs Cooppen's shoes. After all, they would hardly be the sort of thing a mugger would take from the body.
>
> I was looking out all the time for what you could call evidence of system – a pattern in his way of life or in his offending.
>
> I saw from our files that at the beginning of March – just three weeks before Jini Cooppen was killed – Vijay had been driving a Ford saloon car which was involved in an accident with another car.
>
> Rather than face up to the problem he decided he would try to make sure he wasn't traced. He removed the number plates and then reported it missing to local police. The analogy between this and the discovery of his wife's corpse is that both had been stripped of identification. In this case it was clear the hope had been that we would not connect the body in Brixton with the missing person report in Wimbledon.

Had the AMIP system – specifically devised to enable relevant information from across a wide geographical area – not been in place, Vijay Cooppen might have succeeded. As it was, what had been planned as a means of diverting attention from himself had resulted in precisely the opposite.

It was also a car that was to provide the penultimate piece of circumstantial evidence. The forensic science laboratory had been examining the imprint of tyre treads found in the alley-way near Jini Cooppen's body.

Initially the prospects of identification seemed bleak, but then came a breakthrough. The scientists were able to say with complete certainty that the marks were made by a vehicle which had two different brands of tyres – a Goodyear on the front off-side and a Dunlop on the front nearside wheel.

A check on the Cooppen family Volvo showed that it had three Dunlop tyres – and one brand new Goodyear. The latter had been fitted at a local tyre depot on 30 March – the morning of the murder. A visual comparison of the tyre's tread with the marks found in Orphanage Alley appeared to match them perfectly. Bassett thought he was home and dry.

He had not counted on the reluctance of the forensic staff to make a cast-iron guarantee that the two were identical. It was tantalisingly close. To make sure he set about tracing the batch of tyres from which Vijay Cooppen's Goodyear had originated.

> We discovered that there were only twelve moulds in existence which produced that particular type and size of tyre, and of those twelve there were only two which could have produced the particular tread pattern we found on Cooppen's tyre and in the alley. That increased the odds that the mark by the body came from his car.

But increasing the odds was, at this point, not enough. Bassett sent his men back to Goodyear to re-check the tyre details. What they came up with was yet more evidence suggesting that Vijay Cooppen's car had been responsible for the tyre print in the alley.

Most of the tyres produced by the particular moulds in question were destined for export to Holland, where they would be fitted on new Volvos. Only a small percentage was sent out to tyre fitting companies in Britain.

The circumstantial evidence against Vijay was now so strong that John Bassett would have been tempted to charge him on it alone. The final breakthrough came a few days later: Nagaissen Cooppen changed his statement. In a new version, fully witnessed by his uncle, Reuben Pavaday, the 5-year-old boy explained that his father had told him to lie to detectives about Vijay's movements. Specifically, he was instructed to say that they were together at home between 12.00 midnight and 5.00 am on Friday, 30 March – precisely the period within which Jini Cooppen's body was dumped in front of Arch 535, Orphanage Road, Brixton.

Nadesse 'Vijay' Cooppen was charged with murder. He was

convicted on 12 February 1991, and given the mandatory sentence of life imprisonment. Bassett says:

> I think he really believed he had committed the perfect murder. He had gone to such lengths to throw us off the scent – dumping the body elsewhere, removing all identification, playing the part of the worried husband turned grieving widower. He thought he'd done it, got away with it.
>
> But there's no such thing as the perfect murder: however careful the killer has been there will always be a trace of something we can latch on to. And when you come down to it Vijay Cooppen was like almost every other murderer – an amateur. Thank God the jury saw through him and returned the right verdict.

At which point Bassett and the remainder of the AMIP team could smile with satisfaction at a job well done, and begin to sort out the mountain of routine paperwork – overtime claims, internal budgeting, and commendation reports – that are the invariable legacy of a large murder enquiry.

But for the rest of London the conviction of one sadistic wife-beater and killer, though welcome, was rather less a cause for celebration. In February 1991 Chiswick Family Rescue – the world's oldest refuge for abused women – faced up to a financial crisis. Within a month half of its fourteen staff were made redundant, and contingency plans drawn up to shut down some or all of its four separate refuge houses and its vital 24-hour telephone crisis line.

Unless new funding can be found, the already inadequate number of sanctuaries will be reduced by one. There will then be just 199 havens of safety for women like Jini Cooppen, who face the ordeal of violent partners. Sandra Horley, the articulate Canadian who runs the refuge, sees in this a depressing lack of public understanding.

> We have in Britain 1,500 shelters for neglected or cruelly treated animals – and that's a fine thing. But we have trouble maintaining just 200 for abused women, even fifteen years after a Parliamentary Committee said we need 800.
>
> It makes you wonder where people's priorities lie. The

abuse of women takes place all the time – murder is just the
end of a continuum of male violence – yet it seems that this
isn't enough to give the issue of women abuse a high priority.
The only conclusion I can come to is that women just aren't
viewed as important enough to protect.

5
The Crucial Gene

She said, 'Please don't kill me'. I still have
those words in my head: they won't go
away . . . Lord sweet Jesus send me to
Hell.

John Dunne, Brixton, 27 February 1989

Prisoner 3318, John Michael Paul Dunne, was convicted at the Old Bailey of the murder of Lorraine Benson on
Tuesday, 23 October 1989.

He was given the mandatory sentence of life imprisonment.
Mr Justice Waterhouse said: 'It is clear you must not be
released until you are no longer a danger to women.'

He will serve, at most, twenty years in the seclusion of a
secure wing of Albany Prison on the Isle of Wight.

John Michael Paul Dunne will be back on the streets – at the
latest – by the year 2010. And he may well kill again.

Lorraine Benson was by nature a cheerful and outgoing
person. Friends describe her variously as 'lively', 'loud' and
possessing that rare inner happiness which invariably induces
similar feelings in those who came into contact with her.

She had been born in Carshalton, Surrey, on 23 May 1966,
the youngest of three daughters to Michael and Patricia
Benson. Considered a bright child, at school she passed a string
of CSE exams, and developed an extensive interest in an
extremely wide range of academic and practical subjects. 'She

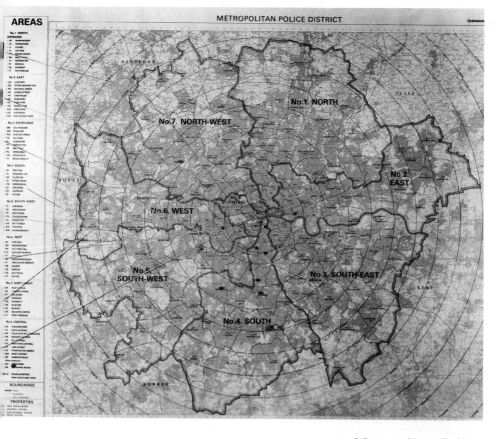

1. Metropolitan Police
Area Map showing
all 8 AMIP territories

METROPOLITAN POLICE
Appeal for Witnesses

MURDER

At about midnight on
Monday 19 December 1988
Lorraine Benson (22)
was brutally murdered in
Cottenham Park Road. She
had walked from Raynes
Park railway station along
Coombe Lane towards the A3.
She wore a white full length
coat and blue jeans.

DID YOU SEE HER?
CAN YOU HELP?

Please contact the Incident Room at

WIMBLEDON POLICE STATION
Tel:- 01-541 1212 or ring

All information treated
as strictly confidential

AP/49B/88

CRIMESTOPPERS
0800 555 111

2a. *above*
Lorraine Benson
2b. *right*
John Michael Paul
Dunne

3a. *left*
Yogannaigaa
'Jini' Cooppen
3b. *below*
Nadesse 'Vijay'
Cooppen

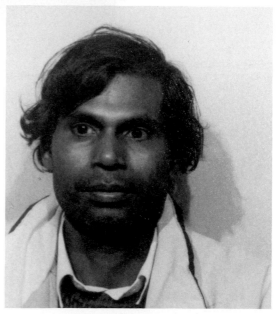

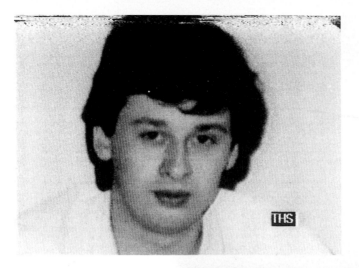

4a. *above*
Noel Christopher
4b. *right*
Brett Simon White
4c. *below*
Adrian Dennis
Williams –
cleared of murder
but convicted of affray

5a. *left*
David Napier
Hamilton
5b. *below*
Kingsley Ignatius
Rotardier

6a. *above*
Chief Superintendent
Bob Chapman, Head
of 4 AMIP, and
Superintendents John
Bassett (left) and
David Fielding.
6b. *right*
Chief Inspector
Peter Elcock

7a. *above* Superintendent Bill Lavers (left) and Inspector David Cooper
7b. *below*
4 AMIP HOLMES Computer Suite

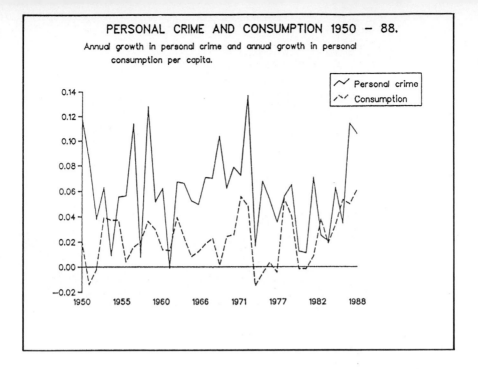

PERSONAL CRIME AND CONSUMPTION 1950 – 88.

Annual growth in personal crime and annual growth in personal consumption per capita.

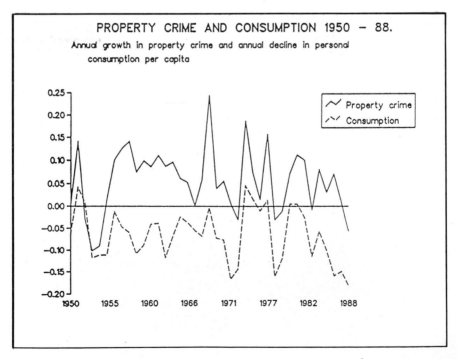

PROPERTY CRIME AND CONSUMPTION 1950 – 88.

Annual growth in property crime and annual decline in personal consumption per capita

8. The Economics of Murder: Home Office graphs highlight the link between homicide and national wealth.

was,' her father recalls, 'interested in almost everything. She had a real depth of general knowledge and always had an opinion about everything. Don't get me wrong, she wasn't a saint and we disagreed about things like any family, but people always found her good to be with.'

The Benson family lived in a comfortable family house in South Norwood. When Lorraine left Pelham High School in South Wimbledon at the age of 16, she worked variously as a waitress and a burger bar server in addition to tackling a typing course to improve her prospects. From each the report on Lorraine Benson was the same: hard-working, friendly, honest and popular with the customers and staff.

One amongst her range of interests was photography and in 1986 she talked herself into a job with a photo processing firm in nearby East Croydon. Although there was no chance to get involved in the technical side of the work, she enjoyed what she was allowed to do.

Glandular fever, an illness which can be severely debilitating, put paid to this first venture in the photographic industry. Lorraine suffered quite badly and for a long period. When she recovered she took on a very different job, working in Switzerland as a nanny for a British couple and their young daughter. Once again her sunny charm won over the family and their friends: letters continued to flow between them long after the job finished.

Back in Britain towards the end of 1986, Lorraine found work in another Croydon photographic shop where, for the first time, she was given training in the technical aspects of the art of photography. But the job didn't last and for more than a year she found herself unemployed.

True to form, she did not sit idle: her sister Tanya had a boyfriend with a carpentry business. Lorraine mucked in and helped out. Eventually, in August 1988, she found herself a job back in the field she knew best: photography.

Like many department stores, Arding and Hobbs at Clapham Junction, a few miles to the north of her home in Wimbledon, leased out space to an independent photographic agency on its sales floors. Pastel Portrait Photography Ltd coped with the bread and butter end of commercial photography – posed snaps of children and babies, and general adult portraiture.

Lorraine Benson was an instant success. Hired initially as a trainee photographer/sales person, her outgoing personality and particular affinity with children complemented a natural talent for photography. She told Michael and Patricia that she felt she had found a vocation – a belief fostered and confirmed when she won a photography competition organised by a national newspaper. Her employers, too, were impressed: promotion to Studio Supervisor was mooted.

Pastel Portrait had another site a few miles south east of Arding and Hobbs. Children's World was situated in Waddon, near Croydon. Periodically Lorraine would be sent over to help out with its child portrait work. One such period began in November 1988, and was – typically – successful. Mick Benson later met one of her satisfied customers.

> I drive a mini-cab for a living and I picked up a woman with a young kid. We got talking and it came out that Lorraine had taken her child's photograph in December that year. She told me how good Lorraine had been with her kid and with some others in the shop. There was a little boy there and he had decided he didn't want his picture taking. Lorraine did her usual one woman show, making noises and so forth and before long the boy was fine about things. She had a real talent for it, a natural affinity with kids.

Life, then, for Lorraine Benson was good. She had a job she loved, a happy home, enough money to spend on the standard round of concerts, ice rinks, night clubs and gymnasia. If she was without a steady boyfriend she was never short of good company for a drink and a laugh.

On Monday, 19 December she had an additional cause for celebration: Arding and Hobbs was to hold its traditional office Christmas Party that night and Lorraine was, quite naturally, invited.

She arrived at Children's World at 10.00 am and began work

immediately. Her shift was due to end at 6.00 pm, and she had told her colleagues with evident pleasure about the party that night. When her replacement arrived, she slipped into the staff rooms at the back of the shop and changed out of the maroon company uniform into a pair of faded Levi 501 jeans, and a yellow blouse and cowboy boots, topped off with a distinctive white coat.

A pre-party drink had been arranged at the Falcon pub near Arding and Hobbs. Lorraine walked from the shop to the railway station at Waddon and caught a train to Clapham Junction.

By the time she reached the pub her friends had already left for the party; Lorraine was not unduly worried, and made her own way up to the store's restaurant where the festivities were to be held.

It was a good party. Lorraine's friends remember her drinking a few beers, dancing, talking and enjoying the Christmas spirit. A few of the younger staff, Lorraine included, walked out on to the roof of the store to smoke a cannabis joint. 'She was merry that night,' they would recall, 'but she wasn't drunk.'

Lorraine Benson had another appointment planned for that night. One of her friends was due to fly out to Australia the next day, and Lorraine wanted to see him off. She had known Peter Cox for some time, and occasionally bought small quantities of cannabis from him. But there was nothing exceptional – much less sexual – in their friendship: it was simply indicative of Lorraine's friendly nature that she wanted to say goodbye to him in person.

Towards the end of the party she called home and told her father she would stay at the house Peter shared with his mother, Lotte, in Raynes Park. She also called Cox to arrange for him to meet her at the station: it would be late when she got there, and she had frequently talked to her friends about her nervousness of walking alone at night. Her fear had not been eased by a series of recent threatening phone calls to her.

At 11.30 pm Lorraine left the party and walked with two

friends to the huge and sprawling confusion of different rail lines that converge at Clapham Junction station. The train which would carry her the few miles across suburbia to Raynes Park arrived at platform 11 ten minutes later. Just as it was ready to pull out another friend hopped on board more than a little unsteady from the night's celebrations. Lorraine, he managed to remember, seemed cheerful and talked about moving back to Arding and Hobbs after Christmas.

It was 11.53 pm when the train rattled in to Raynes Park station. Lorraine and her colleague walked down the cold stone stairs and out on to Kingston Road together. There was no sign of Peter Cox. Lorraine walked on a few yards into Coombe Lane until she found a row of four phone boxes. She slipped inside and dialled Cox's number.

Lotte Cox was a social worker, and had become friendly with Lorraine over the preceding weeks and months. She was also used to Peter's chronic unreliability. She explained that he had not returned from a drinking session, and suggested that Lorraine should begin to make her own way along Coombe Lane to the house in Holland Avenue.

In fact Peter Cox turned up at home fifteen minutes after his mother put the phone down. Lotte Cox was beginning to be worried: it should not have taken so long for Lorraine to arrive. She told Peter his friend would be walking up the road alone: he showed no interest.

But if Peter Cox was not bothered, Lotte was. She took the dog and began searching for Lorraine. She walked up and down the road, but could see no sign of the girl. She walked back home and telephoned the police. Next she got into her car and drove down to the station to check whether Lorraine had gone back there: again she had no luck.

Lotte Cox drove slowly home and, at a little after 1.00 am, phoned Michael Benson to tell him his daughter was missing.

But although Mrs Cox had not seen Lorraine on the road, others had. The distance between Raynes Park railway station and the Cox family home in Holland Avenue is just under a mile. John Davidson, a builder, drove past her at around midnight as she walked along Coombe Lane and past a launderette on one corner. Her white coat particularly attracted his attention.

Fifteen minutes later Brian Laverick, an off-duty bus driver, saw her walking determinedly further down Coombe Lane. Again it was the long white coat which made him notice her. The point at which Mr Laverick saw Lorraine Benson was no more than 150 yards away from Lotte Cox's house. She was nearly safe. But within a minute or so other witnesses would recall seeing her struggle with a man wearing dark clothing.

John McLean was sitting in his lounge that night finishing writing his Christmas cards when he heard a woman's shouts – they seemed angry or exasperated – and then the sound of running feet. Without stopping to put on his shoes he walked through to the front door and stepped out into Coombe Lane. About 50 yards up the road he saw a woman in a long white coat together with a man wearing a dark jacket.

The man was standing almost directly under a bush and was not distinctly identifiable. But Mr McLean could see that the man and the woman had their arms on each other's shoulders. He took them, at first sight, for a courting couple, but then remembered the shouts. He also remembered he had no shoes on his feet, and ducked back inside to fetch them. When he got back to the door the man and the woman had gone.

Alan Fuentis drove his taxi along Coombe Lane a few minutes later. He saw a woman in a white coat standing with her back to a low wall and facing a man who was gesticulating wildly within inches of her face. The woman appeared to be standing very, almost unnaturally still and upright. Mr Fuentis would later say he assumed the man and woman were a couple having an argument.

In fact, Lorraine Benson was terrified: far from being out walking with a boyfriend, as the witnesses assumed, she had been accosted and threatened by an exceedingly violent man. The fact that he appeared to be a little younger than her made it no less frightening.

According to Detective Superintendent Fielding, the AMIP
SIO who was 'next in frame' that night:

> Lorraine was intercepted as she walked along Coombe Lane.
> The witnesses didn't manage to see what happened exactly
> but from what occurred later it is clear that the man
> threatened her or possibly attempted a sexual assault. She
> then ran away, but he caught up with her again near the
> point in Coombe Lane where it joins Holland Avenue. It was
> in an alley-way off there that he started to attack her.

The alley-way in question is a cul-de-sac, 65 feet long, running
behind and roughly parallel to Coombe Lane. Earlier on the
night of Monday 19 December, a red Vauxhall Chevette had
been parked outside the garage at the closed end of the road. It
was still there when, at a little after 12.15 on the Tuesday
morning, Lorraine Benson was dragged down the street.

Her attacker punched her around the head, stunning her
and knocking her against the car. The punches were brutally
effective: Lorraine slumped, semi-conscious, to the ground. The
man picked her up and, clutching her arm, guided her out of
the alley and towards a secluded footpath in nearby
Cottenham Park Road. The distance between the two locations
is a little over a quarter of a mile. At some point on the journey
Lorraine recovered her senses and began to scream and
struggle. The man held her more tightly and steered her
towards the bushes.

A few minutes later two teenage skateboarders, out on
Coombe Lane for a late-night session, heard a succession of
high-pitched screams. They were not alone. A bank clerk,
Kevin O'Rawe, was in bed in his house on Coombe Lane when
the shouting woke him and his wife, Resario.

They realised quickly that the noise was of a woman
screaming in terror. Worse, it continued for at least ten
minutes. The couple went over to the bedroom window to check
whether they could spot the trouble. There was no sign of life
other than the two skateboarders. They listened carefully, and
again the screaming started. It seemed to come from the

direction of the footpath and allotments down by Cottenham Park Road, but neither of them could be sure. Finally the shouting stopped. The O'Rawes went back to bed.

At 1.50 am Lotte Cox and Michael Benson were both talking to Wimbledon police. The circumstances of Lorraine's disappearance – so close to safety and having just phoned Mrs Cox to say she was on her way – made an immediate search of the area the most urgent priority. By 2.00 am as many uniformed officers as the duty inspector could muster were beginning to quarter the streets and alley-ways between Raynes Park Station and Holland Avenue.

At 4.30 am the first significant discovery was made: in the cul-de-sac behind the shops in Coombe Lane a young PC found a plastic carrier bag containing a bra, pants, t-shirt, trousers, shirt, gloves and two small cans of lager. Nearby, a circular metal earring was lying on the ground; several feet away, on the other side of the alley, was its pair; beside it was a packet of Benson and Hedges cigarettes and nearby a man's white handkerchief. The constable noted its presence, together with the fact that it appeared to be stained with blood and mucus. He deliberately did not touch or pick it up: the most mundane of objects can turn out to be vital clues.

It was to take another eight hours before they found Lorraine's body. It was hidden in dense bramble bushes off the path by Cottenham Park Road and someone had attempted to cover it with leaves. The only clothes left in place were a pair of socks and a jumper. The rest appeared to have been torn off and, together with her handbag and jewellery, had been thrown to the winds and lay scattered over a wide area. Some of them had ended up on a makeshift bonfire.

Lorraine Benson had died fighting off her attacker. Although she had been sexually assaulted it was clear she had not been raped. Her left arm was lying defensively across her body, the fingers against her upper thigh. The blood underneath her nails and the bruising on the skin below them pointed to an inescapable conclusion. The verdict of Superintendent David Fielding was:

She had been killed while defending her honour. I think she had been punched on the chin in the alley off Holland Avenue, and dragged half-conscious to the pathway where her attacker had attempted to have sex with her. When she fought back he killed her.

There were quite a number of bloodstained twigs around the body, and we found a sash cord, or rope, nearby which also showed signs of blood. It was pretty clear from the body itself that she had been strangled: the rope looked certain to be the murder weapon.

But it was evident from the marks on the body itself that the attack had been particularly brutal. Obviously there were the sort of scratch marks and defence wounds one would expect, but there were bite-marks as well on the inside of the left arm. Other than to say this indicated an extremely violent attack we couldn't make much sense of those.

If psychological profiling had been more widely available – or at least treated with less scepticism by the police service at large – David Fielding might have found an explanation for the bites, and been able to build up a picture of the killer.

Since the early 1980s psychologists – particularly those working and researching in America – have identified a syndrome evident in some murders which they call 'anger biting'.

Individual case studies revealed a pattern-building – a pattern which showed not just that some murderers felt the need to leave bite-marks on their victims, but that there were probably three different categories of 'bite-killers' at work, all of whom had a different psychological profile. Richard A. Walter, prison psychologist at Michigan Intensive Program Center, explained the phenomenon in a 1984 article for the *American Journal of Forensic Medicine and Pathology*.

Due to a pattern of psychologically expressed ritualism the perpetrator will often inadvertently leave important psychological clues at the crime scene. The attack style, mode of death, characteristics of the victim etc., these components reveal the information on the type of psychological needs that the perpetrator is trying to satisfy.

In the cases of bite-marks associated with violent crime, it becomes crucial to an investigator what type of personality characteristics are welded together to form this kind of need complex.

Three major groups seems to be apparent. The first group is motivated out of an anger track, the second group is motivated out of sadistic biting, and the third is out of the more traditional 'cannibal complex' motif.

Behind the twisted prose style was a simple idea. There is always a motive for an offending action. If the killer takes the trouble to inflict bites on his victim, there has to be a reason. Find the reason and you can come closer first to catching the perpetrator and then to working with him to control his behaviour.

Underneath that simple concept was another, slightly less tangible, notion. Sex offenders – and anger biting is more common in sex offences than other crimes – are frequently meeting a non-sexual need in a sexual way. Again, find the need, understand it, and you have the key to controlling the sex offending.

The three types of anger biter are not difficult to separate in layman's terms. The so-called 'anger-track' offender is one who frequently displays over-aggressive and under-controlled bursts of impulsive anger, often stemming from being unable to handle conflict – and frustration from realising this in-adequacy. His biting tends to be short, sharp and directed at the location of the victim's body which he perceives as being the cause of his immediate problem. For this reason it is not uncommon to find bite-marks on battered babies.

The type and consistency of a sadistic biter's jaw-print is, unsurprisingly, characterised by ripping and tearing marks on the flesh. The aim is power and dominance: the infliction of pain becomes part – a crucial part – of the sexual act, or a sexual act in itself. This type of offender conforms to another pattern: his behaviour is an escalating cycle of sadistic violence, encom-passing fetishism, voyeurism, dominance, bondage and ulti-mately the attainment of sexual satisfaction from stabbing, cutting or biting.

The final anger biter, the possessor of the 'cannibal complex', bites quite literally to absorb his victim's blood. The driving motive is the twisted logic of egomania: by consuming the very essence of his victim's life, the killer is expressing his own supremacy in a way that cannot be questioned, and in some bizarre delusion, perceives himself to be absorbing his 'enemy's' strength.

An analysis of the bite-marks found on Lorraine Benson's body would probably have indicated that her murderer belonged to the second category – a sadistic biter entering the later stages of his compulsion. That, in turn, would have alerted the detectives to examine the previous records of local sex offenders (most sexual killers work within a limited 'patch') who appeared to be following an increasingly sadistic spiral of offending.

But anger biting was not, in 1989, a widely understood phenomenon among British police. Worse, there was no – is still no – central and exhaustive database of sexual offenders available to detectives hunting the perpetrator of a new outrage.

Certainly, the Metropolitan police maintains its own records of convicted paedophiles and rapists. Certainly, the Police National Computer carries details of the offences of those who are sentenced for their sexual crimes. But there is no universal analytical breakdown of these men; nothing that would enable a psychological profile to be matched to a known and established offender's record.

The closest Britain comes to such a system is the dedicated HOLMES suite of powerful computers which is fired up for major operations. But even HOLMES, effectively a huge computerised card index, with the capacity for millions of individual convictions to be recorded in its gigabytes of computer memory, is far from infallible. It will, of course, pick out the most likely suspect for a particular crime, based upon a known *modus operandi*: but it cannot pick up a potential suspect unless that suspect's name and details have been entered in the first place. In case after case HOLMES has failed to identify the offender precisely because his record has not been entered. Typically the reason will be that the offences detailed took place several years before the incident under investigation or, when he was still a teenager. The common theme behind this reasoning is a complete lack of understanding of sexual offending patterns. It does not matter that the offence is historic or committed whilst a juvenile; what matters is evidence of aberrant behaviour.

But although working without the aid of psychological insights and with a potentially flawed database, 4 AMIP had the advantage of considerable expertise in handling murder cases, and the benefit of an operational system which allowed a wide geographical overview of potentially related crimes.

Superintendent David Fielding is a tall, slim man, his silver hair adding a distinguished touch to a face still handsome after a quarter of a century of mopping up society's ills. There is something calming in his manner – quiet, methodical and dependable. For a case that would require an extremely safe pair of hands from day one, David Fielding was an inspired selection.

It was obvious from the scene of the crime that the killing had a sexual motive. Equally, I knew that my colleagues on 5 AMIP in Kingston – which is just a few miles away – were already investigating a series of rapes and attempted rapes going back almost a year.

The attacks had taken place late at night and in secluded or derelict areas close to railways stations. The press had begun to dub the offender 'the railway rapist'.

I couldn't ignore the possibility that whoever killed Lorraine had also been responsible for the two rapes and one attempted rape 5 AMIP was dealing with. I decided pretty quickly that we would work in parallel, in a joint operation.

There were obvious advantages, even though from that first moment I made it clear we could well be looking for different attackers. 4 AMIP was handling six other major investigations at the time, so there was already a shortage of officers.

The Benson case needed a lot of staff and quickly: for several days we had more than seventy officers out working

on the investigation and another fourteen back manning the
office. By running a joint operation based at Wimbledon, I
was able to ease the burden back at Croydon.

This seemingly technical and relatively minor consideration –
whose office, whose men – is just one of the multiplicity of
headaches facing an SIO as he contemplates the beginning of
yet another murder enquiry. As David Fielding made the
logistical arrangements, Dr Stephen Ming Tak Chan formally
pronounced life extinct: the body was taken away to St
George's Hospital, Tooting for post mortem examination.

There remained two major and immediate tasks. The first
was to arrange support and care for Lorraine's family. Fielding
made contact with the Victim Support Scheme, which sent
round a care worker immediately. To supplement this he
appointed Jennifer Wood, a detective constable attached to the
AMIP, as his liaison with the family: it was his procedural way
of asking her to sit with them, help them and relay any
messages or questions they might have back to his desk.

It was essential to maintain close contact throughout, and all
of us went round to the house or rang up almost every day.
Christmas was coming up fast, and I guessed that the
Bensons would need to feel there was someone in the police
who cared, even on Christmas Day.

As it turned out I was right. Mick Benson rang up the
incident room during that Christmas Day. He just wanted to
know that the enquiries were progressing. One of the
detective sergeants was on duty and was able to reassure
him.

There was also the crime scene itself. The area round the
brambles – like the alley-way off Holland Avenue – was
positively littered with Lorraine's clothes and possessions.
Somewhere, on something, there might be a clue – a fingerprint, a blood group: anything to help catch the killer.
Everything was collected, from the car in the alley-way to the
discarded man's handkerchief. Fielding also made a mental
note to have impressions made of the bite-marks on Lorraine's

arms. With witness statements unable accurately to describe the killer, it was going to be up to the scientists to provide identification evidence.

Rufus Thomas began the autopsy later that afternoon. He noted the fact that, although there was evidence of inter- ference with the genital area, Lorraine had not been raped. Equally, the number and type of defensive wounds indicated that she had fought hard to protect herself.

The common features of death by strangulation – the blue lips and ears of cyanosis, the tiny petechiae or haemorrhages across the face and in the eyes – were present, as was the evidence of what had been used to cause asphyxia. Lorraine's neck showed pressure and abrasion marks which suggested that a woven cord had been wrapped round three times and pulled tight. At the back was the impression of the point where the loops had crossed over; at the front a clear tracery of the individual strands of the rope. They matched the sash cord found near the footpath by Cottenham Park Road.

The notion that scene-of-crime evidence can be the key to conviction is not new. It was first articulated in 1910 by the French criminologist, Edmond Locard. He developed, whilst working as an assistant to Professor Alexandre Lacassange, the leading forensic criminologist of the day, a theory he called the 'exchange principle'. The offender in any given crime will always leave something of himself at the scene, or take away minuscule parts of the scene itself when he leaves. Find and examine those bits of exchanged material and science can help convict the criminal. It is this we now know as forensic evidence.

There are, in essence, four main concerns of forensic evidence in murder cases: to identify the victim, the cause of death, and any contributory factors or evidence of other offences, and ultimately to pinpoint the offender. Early experiments in the science tended to be crude: for several centuries attempts at identifying victims relied on displaying their heads in public in the hope that someone might recognise them.

The key to a rather more empirical approach came with the invention of the microscope by Anton van Leeuwenhoek in 1670. Early versions were inevitably crude affairs, but by the beginning of the nineteenth century the microscope had evolved into the familiar shape we know today.

It was the simple power of magnification – something modern science takes for granted – which made all the difference: prior to microscopic analysis the myriad unique characteristics of, for example, an individual hair were unknown because they were beyond the scope of the naked eye. The ability to 'blow up' an image hundredfold made comparison and matching possible.

The first use of the microscope in a murder enquiry was recorded in 1847 by detectives in Paris. They were investigating what would become known as the Praslin Affair: the violent death of Fanny, wife of Duke Choiseul-Praslin.

Initially the police thought she had been killed by burglars: certainly the scene of the murder was suitably chaotic. Not only was there blood quite literally across the walls, sprayed apparently from a gaping neck wound, but the house had been ransacked.

The Duke's evidence seemed to confirm this version of events. He had, he testified, heard his wife cry out, and as a dutiful husband should, had rushed into her bedroom brandishing a pistol. When he saw how badly injured Fanny was, he dropped the gun, fell to his knees and cradled her head in his arms.

But even the relatively unsophisticated forensic scientists of early Victorian Paris were able to detect something odd about the corpse's appearance. In addition to having her throat cut, Fanny had been beaten about the head with a blunt object. Moreover, hypostasis, or lividity, indicated that this had occurred some time before death.

A search of the Duke's own quarters produced a bloodstained handkerchief and dagger – useful, but not conclusive evidence pointing to his involvement. It was at this point that the pistol was put under the microscope. The Duke had explained the presence of blood on the butt by saying he had dropped it before cradling his wife's head. The power of magnification revealed a different story.

Not only was the butt covered in blood, but there was hair stuck to the gore, skin tissue on the trigger guard and combinations of both elsewhere on the weapon. It was clear that the pistol had been used to hit a human head.

The forensic examination provided the final clinching clue which ultimately convicted the Duke. But it was standard detective work which got the case to the point where science could complete the picture. Praslin had been having an affair with a servant: Fanny had found out, threatened divorce and the embarrassment of exposure.

This early case set the pattern for all that followed it. Forensic examination can conclusively trap a killer – but only when that killer has been previously identified.

The next major advance in forensic science came almost thirty years later, when in 1875 a German scientist, Leonard Landois, discovered that all human blood was not the same. A further quarter of a century passed before this landmark discovery was put to practical use.

In 1900 Karl Landsteiner was an assistant professor of medicine in Vienna. He began experimenting with blood to see whether it was possible to divide it into its constituent parts. Using a centrifuge – a simple circular device, much like a miniature fairground ride, which spins a series of test-tubes round at a regulated speed until gravity ceases to effect their contents – he was able to separate out the colourless serum from the red blood cells themselves.

He then tried adding blood cells from different people to his original serum. Sometimes they merged forming the familiar red liquid. But on other occasions they seemed to repel each other like magnets with the same polarity. The result of these experiments was a sludgy porridge-like mixture.

The medical jargon describing this process – 'agglutination' for those cells which bonded with the serum – gave forensic science a new breakthrough. Landsteiner reported that some factor in the serum – he called it agglutinin – reacted against certain blood cells, which he duly termed agglutinogens.

The observation allowed for a straightforward binary test of reactions which would indicate the presence of blood type A, or blood type B. Unfortunately science is rarely that simple: Landsteiner quickly discovered a third category – blood type C – which didn't react precisely like either of its predecessors, instead demonstrating characteristics of both.

From there progress was fast in discovering other variants – notably blood type AB, based on a serum which did not agglutinate with either blood type A or B. At the same time, and less for scientific reasons than administrative convenience, type C blood was renamed type O.

Only one problem remained. Landsteiner's experiments had taken as their core sample human blood, and shown that it was possible to distinguish between differing types. This was crucial to the investigation of murder, where blood was frequently spilled but previously not examined. But no comparable test existed to distinguish between human and animal blood.

In 1901 another German scientist, Paul Uhlenhuth, developed a simple way of telling the difference. Within a year it would be used to convict a French murderer who had tried to explain away the presence of blood on his clothing by saying he had skinned a rabbit. The new test proved him a liar.

This late Victorian work forms the basis of all subsequent blood typing, even the sophisticated and near faultless modern science of 'genetic fingerprinting' – the technique discovered in 1984 and which five years later would help identify the killer of Lorraine Benson.

But the years between the turn of the century and the discovery of DNA genetic fingerprints saw a rash of ever more sensitive tests to type, categorise and evaluate bloodstains. The most important of these was the discovery in the 1920s of sub-groups of the basic blood types. Statistical analysis showed that 40 per cent of the world's population are type A, 40 per cent type O, 15 per cent type B, and 5 per cent type AB.

Given the high statistical chance that both killer and victim would be of the same blood group, the science of serology was stalled. But prolonged and patient experimentation showed first that type A blood sub-divided into two groups of identical characteristics, but different strengths, then that there were two more distinct blood groups, M and N. Finally, a series of experiments using rhesus monkeys identified a particular type variant which distinguished otherwise identical samples of blood from the major groups: the rhesus sub-type or 'factor' was added to the pantheon.

In 1949 another refinement enabled scientists to distinguish between male and female blood by the isolation of nuclei within the cells which are unique to women.

All of this now meant that when blood was discovered at the scene of a crime it could be tested to determine whether its origin was animal or human, male or female and what identifying group it belonged to. From the initial two main groups discovered by Landsteiner, serologists can now place samples with certainty into one of 288 different types.

Furthermore, serology has proved that more than 80 per cent of the population are 'secretors' – their blood cells are present in other body fluids such a saliva or semen: which makes it possible to determine the blood type of, for example, a rapist from the evidence of his crime.

But serology has always been something of a cinderella science in the otherwise glamorous world of forensic criminology where the studies of ballistics, toxins, fibres and hairs have traditionally been deemed paramount. This is partially due to its resolutely medical nature – whereas other forensic disciplines do not necessarily require intense medical study and qualifications, serology is grounded in the most basic of medicine – and partly due to the fictional representation of fingerprinting as the single greatest of all scientific advances.

Certainly, the development of a reliable identifying test for habitual criminals was long overdue when, in the 1870s, French police began using the new science of photography as an aide.

The problem with this was not merely that it took fifteen minutes to take one picture, but that there was no way of assembling a database which could be usefully consulted: how, after all, were facial characteristics caught on celluloid to be categorised in a card index?

The initial breakthrough came with the use of anthropometry. In 1875 Alphonse Bertillon was 26 years old, a clerk in the clerical office of the Prefecture of Police in Paris, and bored. To relieve the tedium of the French obsession with minutely-regulated bureaucracy he began experimenting with an early form of photo-fit pictures, simply slicing them into strips and jig-sawing them into 'new' faces.

Behind this apparent parlour game was a serious intent. Bertillon had read and found fascinating a treatise by a Belgian astronomer, Lambert Quételet, entitled 'Anthropometry – Or The Measure Of Different Faculties In Man'.

The basis of the idea was to apply the science of statistics to the measurement of bodily features, since no two human beings have precisely the same measurements. Bertillon decided that this could form the basis of a much-needed system to identify convicted criminals, and devised a rigorously complicated filing system based on minute measurements and cross-references. Thus, and at its simplest, a prisoner with a head 200cm wide, would be filed in the filing drawer marked 200.

When Bertillon put this plan to the Prefect – the equivalent of the early Commissioners at Scotland Yard – he was met with outright hostility: was Monsieur, perhaps, playing a practical joke?, asked the Prefect.

It took until November 1882 to wear the Prefect down. And when he did accede to the clerk's suggestion it was for a limited period only: Bertillon was given three months to prove his system worked. If during that period he could identify one habitual criminal, the experiment would be given an extended lease of life.

Supported by just two clerks, he set to work, working on eleven separate measurements of areas of the body. Statistically the chances of any two men having all eleven identical measurements worked out at four million to one. To back this up he added a photograph to the index card and what he called a *'portrait parlé'* – a written description of any identifying marks such as tattoos, scars or moles.

But the system was too sensitive to be administratively feasible. As each criminal came into the prefecture he would be measured and photographed and a card completed for each of the eleven identifying measurements. The sheer volume of card indexes and filing cabinets this began to consume forced Bertillon to drop from eleven to four basic measurements.

The three-month trial period was almost over before Bertillon's system enabled the arrest of a known offender. When it did, however, the prefecture adopted 'Bertillonage' wholeheartedly and, by 1888, a new Department of Judicial Identity had been established within it. Inevitably Bertillon was appointed its head.

For the next decade Bertillon, and the system he had devised to identify criminals, became famous throughout Europe and the rest of the world. Bertillonage became accepted as the standard identity test, and individual police departments from Paris to La Plata, Nantes to Nepal, set up specialist sections to measure and record the dimensions of those they arrested.

The problem lay in that clerical efficiency – or rather the potential lack of it. So crude was Bertillonage that a minute mistake by a bored office worker could destroy the value of an entire record system.

The answer to the urgent need for a reliable identification process had been known for several hundred years and was, even as Bertillon basked in the glory of his invention, under spasmodic development by gifted – if uncooperative – amateurs around the globe.

The Chinese had been the first nation to recognise that every individual has unique patterns of skin at the end of their fingers and thumbs: many centuries before the invention of the forensic scientist's most basic tool, the microscope, thumb impressions were used to seal important Chinese documents.

The notion that accidental fingerprints – as opposed to deliberately-inked impressions – might have a scientific use dated back to the seventeenth century and the delineation of ridge marks by academic anatomists.

The idea was based on the realisation that, far from acting as a hermetic seal, the skin over the tips of the fingers and thumbs is perforated by literally thousands of holes, or sweat pores. From these a fatty secretion leaks into the maze of papillary lines and, if touched or pressed against another surface, causes a latent print to be made.

But although unique the prints are dazzlingly complicated. Comparison of one to another is quite possible by the naked eye: to look for one particular pattern in a collection of millions is utterly impractical. A method was needed to classify the marks into definable categories.

The first real work on developing such a system began in Calcutta. William Herschel, an English civil servant turned colonial magistrate, found that Indian pensioners were collecting their benefits more than once by simply pretending to be someone else. Herschel dropped on the idea of requiring a finger-print on each receipt. The problem of classification remained, but the prospect of discovery caused a rapid drop in the number of bogus claims.

By 1877 the system was working sufficiently well for Herschel to suggest its wider adoption to the Inspector General of Prisons in Bengal. The idea was summarily rejected.

Simultaneously, a Scottish doctor living in Tokyo, Henry Faulds, had developed a crude way of classifying fingerprints, and had chalked up at least one successful conviction as a result. In October 1880 he outlined his theories in the scientific journal, *Nature*.

Herschel, now back in England, was outraged. He promptly wrote to the magazine explaining that he had first developed the concept of fingerprinting. Faulds, in turn, accused Herschel of attempting to steal his ideas. He stormed back to England and into Scotland Yard where he tried in vain to interest the Metropolitan Police in his invention. The clash and the official inertia were both symptomatic of the bumbling inefficiency of criminological research of the period.

It would take until 1891 for the potential of fingerprinting to begin to be realised. Sir Francis Galton, established as an eminent and respectable scientist, had spent three years studying the nature of the papillary lines. He noticed that most centred around a triangular shape somewhere on the finger pad. Galton took this triangle – he called it by the Greek letter 'delta' – and used it as the basis for all further analysis. The rest of the lines he identified as 'loops' and 'whorls' – thus accurately describing the pattern they formed on any given print.

At this point Galton got stuck. He could see no easy way of classifying the variety of patterns further. But his work was enough to spark the usually somnolent Home Office into life.

The Home Secretary, Herbert Asquith, had been about to sanction the first foray into Bertillonage at Scotland Yard. But Galton's research seemed to offer the prospect of a less complicated system of identification. In the way of all Home Secretaries before and after him, he appointed a committee to re-research what Galton had already researched. Heading it was a civil servant, Charles Troup; with him were Sir Arthur Griffiths, author of the excitable *Mysteries of Police and Crime* and Sir Melville McNaughten, Assistant Chief Constable of the Metropolitan Police. The committee was a classic example of British bureaucratic dithering: it came to few conclusions, none of them practical.

Inevitably, the breakthrough, when it came, happened far away from Britain. Juan Vucetich was head of the statistical bureau of La Plata Police in Argentina. His country had been among the first outside Europe to adopt Bertillonage, and the first thereafter to spot its limitations. Vucetich began work on a reliable classification of fingerprints, based on the ground-breaking research Galton had pioneered alone. It did not take him long to break down the delta patterns into four distinct types. There were those with no triangle, those with a triangle on the right, those with it on the left, and those who had two triangles. It was simple to label these one to four, and similarly identify thumb patterns from A to D. Within a year he had solved a murder with the aid of his new system.

All the time the Troup committee was solemnly getting nowhere, Vucetich was surging ahead. Nor was he alone. In India another civil servant, Edward Henry, solved the problem of a simple classification system based on the number of papillary lines. Henry saw that once the delta had been found all that was needed was to draw a line from what he called its 'inner terminus', through its 'outer terminus' and count the number of lines between the two.

The Henry system, invented in 1895 and adopted through-out India two years later, is the basis of all modern fingerprint classification. Its key was simplicity.

But as with all innovation, crime rapidly overtook the new investigative tool. It did not take much imagination for a criminal to wear gloves, thus denying his pursuers the benefit of his prints. (Although it is now possible to take prints from the inside of the fingers of some gloves.) Almost a hundred years after the invention of what was thought to be the ultimate scientific detection tool, less than 2 per cent of all British criminal investigations are solved by fingerprint evidence.

What was needed was a breakthrough which combined the uniqueness of fingerprint identifications with the undisguis-able characteristics of blood and other bodily fluids. In 1984 it arrived.

Every human body contains approximately a hundred million individual cells, each made up in the same way, of a nucleus surrounded by a protein. The substance which makes up that nucleus is known as nucleic acid.

As early as 1911 it was discovered that nucleic acid comes in two distinct types: the difference between the two is whether they contain a substance called ribose, or one called dexyribose. The labels given to these tell-tale acid types were RNA for those with ribose, DNA for those with dexyribose.

The dexyribose, or DNA, is the most important genetic material in the body. Inside every single cell there are forty-six thread-like objects called chromosomes – twenty-three from the mother's input, twenty-three from the father's. These chromosomes are composed of DNA.

By the Second World War it was clear that DNA was the key building block of all human life – the substance which determines how we look, how we grow, what we will, when we are babies, become. Hair colour, eye colour, height, weight, facial characteristics, body defects or deformities, are all determined by the DNA information carried within the cells. And, with the sole exception of twins, every single human being has different DNA characteristics or codes.

Within a decade British science had cracked the nature of this coding. DNA forms itself into a double-helix pattern made up of four chemicals in a variety of permutations. It is the relative positioning of these chemicals – adenine, guanine, cytosine and thymine – that decides the unique make-up of an individual's chromosomes.

Of course, not all DNA strings are different. Since the substance carries the information that determines the very physical characteristics which make all humans – two arms, two legs, one head etc. – then clearly some lengthy sections have to be the same for everybody. But it is the other sections –dubbed by scientists 'hypervariable regions' – which are crucial: their unique chemical permutations decide how we look and grow differently from other people.

In September 1984, Dr Alec Jeffries was working in a laboratory at Leicester University on identifying the genetic coding of myoglobin proteins – those which carry oxygen to the muscles. During this research he came across a building block made up of repeated sequences within the DNA itself. By isolating the DNA, slicing it into small pieces with a chemical catalyst, adding radioactive probes and then taking photographs with radio-sensitive film, he was able to read the unique biochemical messages much as a supermarket check-out can read the bar codes on food packaging.

Dr Jeffries's startling finding was in the odds against two people having the same DNA bar code – 1,000,000,000,000,000,

000,000,000,000,000,000 to one. The genetic fingerprint had
been discovered. Within three years it had helped convict
offenders from burglars to murderers.

Initially most DNA testing throughout Britain was done by a
handful of private contract laboratories, but in December 1988
the Metropolitan Police Forensic Science service in Lambeth
added genetic fingerprinting to its armoury of technology.
According to Julie Allard of the laboratory staff, the move had
both advantages and drawbacks.

> The advantages of in-house testing were enormous – urgent
> samples could be dealt with immediately, there was direct
> communication with the DNA scientists and there were no
> problems with transport and continuity in transferring
> samples to the commercial labs in Abingdon. But our
> newly-established DNA unit was quickly put under
> considerable pressure.

In large part that pressure was due to the demands of
Superintendent David Fielding at 4 AMIP, and his colleagues
in neighbouring 5 area:

> We were dealing at the same time with the murder and the
> series of rapes or attempted rapes in the Kingston area. They
> had all taken place between 21 October and the day that
> Lorraine Benson died.
>   In fact one of them happened within twenty-four hours of
> Lorraine being strangled. The radius of all the attacks was
> just two-and-a-half miles, three out of four took place in
> alley-ways or secluded places; all happened around midnight
> in the vicinity of railway stations. That's why I decided we
> should work as a joint team when the Benson murder was
> referred to me. I couldn't be certain the crimes were linked –
> but then again I couldn't rule it out.

In fact, in those early days of the investigation David Fielding
had precious little to go on: no reliable witness descriptions, no
fingerprints, no informants. Aside from routine house-to-
house enquiries the only options were speculative forensic tests
on the bits of evidence found at the two places where Lorraine

had been attacked, and appeals via the press for more information.

The first item to arrive at the Lambeth laboratory was the Vauxhall car found in the alley-way behind the Coombe Lane shops. By 20 December it was undergoing extensive tests to check whether any unusual marks or foreign substances had stuck to its paintwork. Julie Allard was involved from the start.

> The car was checked primarily for fingerprints, but the dust marks on the driver's door were also of interest to us. They clearly showed that something had brushed against the door and disturbed the dust: but their zigzag-lined appearance was a puzzle.
>
> It was only a few weeks later, while Lorraine Benson's raincoat was lying on the laboratory bench that the puzzle was solved. The teeth on the zip of her coat could have made the lines by rubbing against the door. We experimented to try the theory out: the tests confirmed it.

Now the scientists were able to tell the detectives that they had evidence of a struggle taking place beside the car. Additionally they were able to report that some of the zigzag lines in the dust did not match the teeth-pattern of Lorraine's coat. It was a logical deduction that they would match those on the coat worn by her killer. It was not the sort of clue to help them track him down, but it would add to the weight of evidence against whoever the detectives finally arrested.

Immediately the AMIP set to work tracing the manufacturer of the mystery zip. Tasks like this in a murder enquiry can seem akin to searching for a needle in a haystack – but experienced SIOs like Fielding know that even the slimmest chances can produce the vital lead.

This time the search ended in frustration. The zip-maker was ultimately found – but the sheer volume of zips he produced and distributed made the prospect of tracking the killer by the fastening of his coat so remote as to be pointless.

A further fifty-nine separate items arrived at the laboratory over the ensuing weeks. Most were objects recovered from the alley-way or the path. They, and with them subsequent swabs taken from the victim's body, were first analysed using conventional serology techniques. The first to be tested was the handkerchief found near the Vauxhall car in the alley-way where Lorraine had first been attacked.

> It was a clean, folded man's handerchief with several stains of diluted blood, some of which we found to be mixed with saliva. Also on the handkerchief was a yellow crusty stain.
>
> Microscopic examination revealed that this was probably nasal in origin, since mucus and large clumps of leukocytes were present. This stain was unsuitable for conventional grouping techniques but ideal for DNA profiling due to the large amount of nuclear material.

Further DNA testing proved that the mucus on the handkerchief was not Lorraine's, though the bloodstains were. The genetic fingerprint of the nasal material was logged: it would be compared with intimate samples taken from any suspects the AMIP brought in.

This process of testing against the scientific certainty of DNA produced one concrete piece of evidence: the man whose DNA was on the handkerchief was not responsible for the Kingston rapes. David Fielding knew then he was looking for a second man.

Meanwhile, he had begun to use his only other option – media coverage. It is a frequent reaction among consumers of television news when grieving relatives of murder victims are shown at a press conference, to criticise the insensitivity of such a ploy.

In fact detectives use the broadcast media and the press as much as they can. Each AMIP is assigned its own dedicated press officer to liaise between the two and obtain as much coverage as possible. Fielding and his colleagues know that television appeals and keeping the murder fresh in the public's mind can yield extra – and vital – clues. He recalls,

> Lorraine died just before Christmas and we tried very hard to get media interest. But within a couple of weeks first

Lockerbie and then the Kegworth air disasters happened,
wiping other – seemingly smaller – deaths off the screen and
out of the newspapers.

Nonetheless, the detectives persevered and evidently had
some success: throughout the time the investigation was
running, the AMIP logged no fewer than 1,375 separate phone
calls offering information. These led to detectives taking 411
individual statements, and ultimately arresting 67 people. Of
them all but one were released after being eliminated from the
enquiry. The one remaining suspect would shortly be charged
with murder.

The circumstances in which Fielding came face to face with
the killer of Lorraine Benson were classic of their kind. At 2.00
am on Thursday, 2 February 1989 – nearly two months after
the murder enquiry began – a 30-year-old computer operator
was nearly raped in Durham Road, Raynes Park. The pattern
of the attempted rape seemed to fit the known behaviour of the
Benson killer: the case was quickly referred to David Fielding.

It is standard procedure in incidents such as this for the
Police National Computer to be checked for details of all sex
offenders living or staying close to the scene of the attack: men
who sexually abuse women or children quite frequently do so
within a limited radius of their own homes.

Almost immediately the computer threw up the name of a
19-year-old youth with a known history of rape, who lived a
few streets away in Amity Grove. At 1.30 pm the same day he
was arrested.

There is much still unknown about the short life of John
Michael Paul Dunne. What little is recorded, however, is far
from comforting. He was born on 25 February 1969, the
youngest of four children. He grew up within an unremarkable
South London family, attending local schools until he reached
the age of 15.

Behind this façade of normality, however, all was far from
well. From the age of 7 he had begun stealing from his family –
a petty offence, but, nonetheless, one to worry his parents.

It was in 1983, when he was 14, that John Dunne's criminal

behaviour took a more sinister turn. He carried out what seemed at first sight to be a straightforward robbery. Closer examination suggested there was an ill-defined sexual motive for the attack – a suspicion which deepened when his long-suffering mother caught him 'peeping' at women while they undressed in a local maternity clinic.

The following year he carried out his first rape. He was convicted and sent to the Glenthorne Youth Treatment Centre in Birmingham for three years.

Lorraine Benson's life might, conceivably, not have been at risk had the regime at Glenthorne attacked the problem of Dunne's offending. Men – and youths – who attack women for sex do so for a reason (or more usually for a complex web of reasons). There is no such thing as a motiveless sex attack.

Most sexual offending follows a definable pattern, often escalating into a cycle of ever-more aberrant behaviour. It is possible to interrupt this cycle using an intensive therapy process.†

Glenthorne – and it was not alone – had no such programme to offer. John Dunne's psychiatrist noted at the end of the three-year sentence that he had not been able to see any change in the youth's sexual attitude and with the sentence completed he had no power to detain him further. This meant that Dunne was on a fast-track to repeating his offences, and there was nothing Glenthorne could now do to stop him.

And so it proved. He continued his peeping-tom sessions, was caught by local police in Amity Grove at 2.00 am one morning with a craft knife and a pair of knotted shoelaces, and displayed a general air of discomfort and menace whenever he came into contact with women. He hung around in bars and pubs, earning a reputation as a nuisance and a weirdo, but picking up occasional work as a glass collector. In one bar, where strippers performed a nightly turn, John Dunne would resolutely turn his back on the act and refuse to watch as a succession of wary and weary women removed layers of

† Ray's work at Gracewell being the best example of this.

impractical underwear to an otherwise favourable male response.

John Dunne fitted the bill for both the attempted rape in Durham Road and the murder of Lorraine Benson six weeks before. On the basis of a successful identity parade before the victim of the sexual assault, and conclusive fingerprint evidence, Fielding decided to charge him with the lesser offence and begin work on investigating any possible link with the murder.

Under the Police and Criminal Evidence Act, he had the right to have intimate samples taken from his suspect with or without consent. As it turned out John Dunne agreed without demur.

Immediately dental impressions, nasal swabs and blood tests were taken and rushed to the Lambeth laboratory. And then began the traditional interviewing which is the basis of all detective work.

Fielding arranged for his most senior deputy, Inspector Arthur 'Abie' Benham, and two detective constables – Gerald Woolmore and Gary Shorricks – to begin interrogating Dunne. Throughout five long and tape recorded interviews he denied any knowledge of the killing of Lorraine Benson.

The laboratory meanwhile was working overtime to assess the body samples which had arrived from Croydon. DNA testing was carried out on all of them, and the results proved spectacular. Fielding explains:

> The lab was able to show that the genetic profiling of the mucus on the handkerchief found in the alley-way off Holland Avenue produced a frequency of one in 1,497,000.
> In simple terms this meant that only forty people in the white population could have had this type of profiling – that was as close as they could get to isolating the individual characteristics. But of that forty half would be women. So we were left with the information that of all the white men in Britain only twenty could have produced this DNA profile. And John Dunne's voluntarily-given intimate samples matched it perfectly.

On 17 February 1989, John Dunne was charged with the murder of Lorraine Benson. He denied the allegation once again. But later the same evening he began to open up to the two detective constables who had been with him since the start of his interrogation.

He began to remember vague details of the day Lorraine died, and Gerald Woolmore was only too happy to encourage him further.

John Dunne had spent the afternoon and evening of Monday 19 December getting stoned out of his head. He had begun at lunchtime, buying a 'purple heart' (amphetamine) tablet in the leisure centre arcade at Kingston. He washed it down with a liberal measure of 'Hell Raisers' – vicious combinations of lager, cider, rum and whisky. He could not recall how, or when, he got from Kingston to Coombe Lane, but when Woolmore drew a sketch map of the area, he confirmed that he had been within 40 yards of where Lorraine was first attacked.

> Gerry Woolmore and Gary Shorricks did a terrific job, getting to know Dunne and gaining his trust. At one point during this informal conversation he turned to Gerry and said: 'My dad thought I'd done it. He said I'd be back [in prison] for good.'
>
> Because of the restrictions of the Police and Criminal Evidence Act, Gerry had to end the interview straight away. Since it came in back in 1986, when we want to question a suspect about a particular crime we have formally to tell him we suspect him of it. If we don't do that then whatever is said can't be used as evidence in court.
>
> Gerry came and told me what Dunne had said and I decided to go back and re-interview Dunne under caution as the law required, and in the presence of his solicitor. It was at this point he made a statement which, though it didn't amount to a murder confession, at least put him in the right place at the right time.

Coupled with the DNA profiling and the results of odontology tests which matched the bite-marks on Lorraine's body to the impressions taken of Dunne's teeth, the detective knew he had won. Fielding was able to tell Mick Benson he had enough to convict the man who killed his daughter.

This in itself was no ordinary courtesy call to a bereaved
relative, but rather a reflection of the special friendship which
had grown up between the two men, matched by a commitment
felt by every member of the investigative team. Their deter-
mination and effort moved Lorraine's parents.

> The police were fantastic to us from the start. They came and
> talked to us, they kept us informed, they were there when we
> needed them. They all seemed to feel Lorraine's death
> personally and they put so much of themselves into finding
> the man who killed her. I can't speak highly enough of them.

At the same time as supporting the Bensons, Fielding – and
particularly Woolmore and Shorricks – were simultaneously
trying to keep on friendly terms with the man they were
convinced had killed the young woman. It was a difficult
balancing act.

Ultimately, their patience was rewarded. On 27 February
Dunne was taken from Brixton to Wimbledon for an identity
parade on another case of indecent assault. Because he had a
court appearance the next day, he was kept in the cells
overnight. Shorricks and Woolmore knew that in the spartan
surroundings of a police cell he would not be in a position to look
his best for the court. They brought him a cleanly laundered
shirt and socks, and left him to change.

This gesture of concern seemed to break through some
psychological barrier. At 9.30 that morning John Dunne
handed the two officers a handwritten and signed confession to
the murder of Lorraine Benson:

> To Gerry and Gary. I sorry [sic] that I couldn't tell. But the
> only [way] I found possible was in writing. Here is my
> confession. All I hope is that God will forgive me for what I
> done . . .

What followed – though in it Dunne admitted his guilt –
was actually a rambling attempt, typical of many sex
offenders, to suggest that Lorraine had, at first, almost invited
his sexual advances, but then changed her mind.

> I thought and mistook [this] as a come-on from her so I
> started to kiss her . . . so I tried to have it off with her. As I did
> so she pushed me away [and] slap me hard in the face. I lost
> control by hitting her to the ground and pulling her over to
> the car where we struggled for about five minutes.

David Fielding still reacts angrily to the points in Dunne's
confession where he alleges that Lorraine agreed to have sex
with him provided he did not kill her.

> I don't accept that at all. Dunne was just making it up to
> justify to himself what he had done. All the evidence showed
> that Lorraine had fought hard to preserve her honour and
> that is how she died.

For Dunne the death was probably a logical end to his pattern
of offending – a way of silencing his victim, rather than as with
other sex killers, part of a calculated act designed to bring
sexual release.

> She screamed and I got frightened and there was a piece of
> rope nearby so I put [it] around her neck just to fright [sic]
> her. I didn't know that I pulled so tight and I don't know how
> long it was for.
> I got down on my knees and rolled her over. She wasn't
> breathing . . . and in a panic I pick her clothes up and chuck
> them all over the place.
> I then run home and got indoors and I went to bed, but I
> couldn't sleep. I still have those words in my head – 'Please
> don't kill me'. They will never go away not even when I am
> dead.
> I just hope God will forgive me for what I have done . . . May
> the Lord sweet Jesus send me to Hell.

The Almighty may one day forgive John Dunne, but Mick
Benson never will: 'I can't understand why we ever got rid of
the death penalty. That's all that slime like him deserve. He
has forfeited the right to life.'
On 23 October 1989, John Michael Paul Dunne forfeited the
right to live outside prison for what the judge called 'life' –
though in reality that means an average of twenty years.
But John Dunne has been to prison before for sexual

offending, and it did not control his cycle of rape and abusing. Which is not, perhaps, very surprising.

The Home Office had, until last year, rested its hopes of changing an offender's behaviour on the assumption that locking him in a Victorian cell with his own chamber pot and a varied selection of other abusers would ensure future compliance with the law. It was a faith as foolish as it was negligent.

In 1991 it announced a new plan to set up six intensive therapy prison units for sex offenders, and to staff them appropriately. Albany Prison, the Category A – top security – jail which currently houses Dunne, will be one of them.

But how genuine is this commitment to change? Some senior officials admit in private that it is as much a cosmetic political exercise, designed to leave the impression that something is being done, rather than a genuine attempt at reform.

We contacted John Dunne to ask for an interview, and to ask above all whether he would be prepared to explore with Ray the reasons for his offending and the possibility of finding a way to control it. It was not a fanciful notion: the Gracewell Clinic takes on such cases day in and day out, generally with a great deal of success.

After consulting his external counsellor Dunne agreed, in writing and with some eagerness. He asked us to arrange a special visiting order from the Home Office. We explained in writing and at length to the Home Office the nature of the request and its potential benefit to Dunne himself.

But the Home Office declined to let either of us in to Albany Prison to see and interview John Dunne. At first it would not give a reason for its refusal, nor say whether or not Dunne was receiving any psycho-sexual therapy. Ultimately, it explained that the doors would remain closed to us because it felt that added publicity would only upset Lorraine Benson's family.

Certainly Mick and Patricia Benson were upset – but not at the prospect of extra column inches. Their ire had been directed at Whitehall for some months after first being offered £650 by the Criminal Injuries Compensation Board as the officially

designated cost of their daughter's life, and then when they
discovered that the explicit written statements and medical
evidence of Lorraine's ordeal would be available to Dunne in
prison.

> We know that this sort of document has a value as currency
> among these sort of offenders – they use them as barter.
> Dunne will be making use of our daughter even after she is
> dead.

Sadly, Mick Benson is right. Such statements, containing
brutally graphic accounts of sexual molestation and death,
function as a sort of pornography amongst the segregated
'Rule 43' sex offenders. There is no reason for the men to retain
these in prison after their lawyers have checked the contents.
The Home Office knows this: only its inertia prevents the
ending of the practice.

But above all it was the lack of any attempt at controlling
Dunne's offending earlier which rankles with Mick Benson.

> When they released him from Glenthorne they knew he
> wasn't safe, they knew he was likely to do something like that
> again, and he did. Lorraine died as a result. That is just plain
> wrong.

Treatment programmes, like those at Gracewell, can
successfully control – if not cure – the behaviour of sexual
offenders. We will examine the nature and scope of this type of
treatment when we come to assess the need for changes in
criminal justice policy and practice in Chapter Eight.

But for now John Dunne remains behind the concrete and
wire of Albany Prison. Will he get the therapy which is the only
chance of breaking his vicious cycle of offending and protecting
the public upon his release? Certainly, the prison has
psychiatrists available to work with him, though only if he
requests their help. Has he made such a request in the two
years he has been there? We shall never know. The Home
Office will not discuss the question of treatment with anyone

outside the prison. It would appear that within Whitehall secrecy is more important than public safety.

6
The Fatal Look

A few words were said, the scuffle broke
out and on the spur of the moment I
seemed to have stabbed some young chap
in the stomach.

*Brett White, South Norwood, 1 January
1990*

The murder of Noel Alan Christopher encapsulated and mirrored the ills of an era. His death was symbolic of the ten-year political upheaval of Thatcherism.

Brett Simon White, too, is a symbol of his time: arrogant and uncaring, casually violent and financially stable.

The life of Brett White and the death of Noel Christopher so neatly sum up the prevailing social dynamics of the 1980s – the age of the designer hooligan both on the terraces and in the City – that it seems only fitting that the one should murder the other on the last day of the last month of the last year of the decade.

This is not an ideological interpretation, but a sociological reality confirmed by the Home Office itself and is one of the ill-understood realities of murder: when the good times roll (for some at least), homicide rises.

Statistics show that the single most common group of homicide victims are children under the age of one. Thereafter the most dangerous age and sex to be is 16 to 24 years old and male.

A Home Office research study covering the unlawful killing

statistics for 1986 showed that 100 more men than women were homicide victims. Of all the men, the majority were within that eight-year age range.

In 1987, the last year for which comparative analysis is available, there was a risk factor of almost 30 per cent for men in this age band as compared to approximately 12 per cent for women. Both sexes at these ages were the most vulnerable to what the Home Office delicately terms 'personal crime'.

Stripped of its scientific language what this study shows is that throughout England and Wales almost three in every hundred men between 16 and 24 will become victims of assaults so serious they either will, or will be lucky not to, lead to death.

The single most common method of administering that violence is via a short sharp blade: 32 per cent of all male homicide victims die from knife wounds. Kicks and blows are the second most popular choice of inflicting death, with a combined rating of 22 per cent.

These are curiously unrecognised facts in the public arena. Perhaps because vicious murders of physically frail old age pensioners make better headlines, there is a popular myth that it is frail senior citizens rather than the young and healthy who need live in fear of violent and murderous assault.

In fact the most dangerous years are those between adolescence and early adulthood, and the most dangerous place to enjoy them – and especially for men – is in the pub, club or nightspot. In London.

Noel Christopher was not a regular drinker. He rarely went out at night, and seemed less enthralled by the pub-club routine of many young men of his age and status. A gentle man, 6 feet tall but with a history of having been bullied at school, his passion was for animals. His elder sister, Gloria, recalls:

> Not content with cats, dogs, birds and chickens, Noel also
> kept an African Grey Parrot and a pet ferret called Snoopy.
> As a child he even arrived home with a snake.

Children loved him and were always knocking on our front
door with birds with broken wings for Noel to look after. He
was a kind and thoughtful person, never too busy to help
mend a neighbour's car or do a favour for a friend.

He always wanted to become a vet, but unfortunately
never did well enough at school to go to university . . . He was
always happier playing with his animals at home than being
in the classroom.

Noel's former girlfriend, Michelle Castle, also remembers
him as a gentle and unassuming man.

Throughout the whole of the period that I knew Noel – about
eight years – he was a shy, quiet and considerate boy. He
never liked going out to clubs or pubs or anything like that.

The reason why we split up was because I wanted to start
going out a bit more, but Noel just never wanted any
nightlife. Throughout the entire period we went out he never
laid a finger on me; he never once got into a fight, or anything
approaching a fight.

He was the sort of person who did not attract trouble – with
the exception of once when he was mugged on his way home
from work. He really was a shy, quiet, kind person who
wouldn't hurt a fly, and just never got involved in fighting or
anything like that.

Noel Alan Christopher was born on 18 December 1964. His
mother was ill for most of his life and it was to Gloria, ten years
older than her brother, that Noel turned in times of trouble.

With his father Noel shared a passion for wildlife and when
in 1986 his mother died, the two men became closer. Gloria was
now married with children of her own; Noel stayed on at home.

Initially he found work with a large London bookstore; when
that job ended he found new employment as a delivery van
driver. His passion for animals remained, supplemented by a
new love – his motorbike. Even though he was in work, and
therefore in funds, Noel was still a reluctant socialite. It was a
rare event for him to be seen out late in a disco, pub or club.

The Saturday of 30 December 1989, was just such a special
occasion. In addition to celebrating the approaching end of the

decade, Noel Christopher was planning a night out in recognition of a friend's 27th birthday.

Alan Peckham had been at school with Noel, and now worked as a labourer. The pair had also been friendly with Jerome Collins, the son of his boss since primary school days, who was now working as a postman.

John Redai, a site agent from New Zealand whom Alan had met in the course of his work, was also included in the party, and invited to meet the three schoolfriends at the Corner Pin pub near Wimbledon Dog Track. From here the plan was to go on to a nightclub called Nelson's, a little further down the road inside Wimbledon Football Club. Alan Peckham had arranged for a fifth friend, a carpenter called Brian Gallagher, to join the group there.

It is worthwhile, given what was to follow, to examine the known history of the five men who gathered that night to celebrate Alan Peckham's birthday: certainly that task would be one of the earliest enquiries made by 4 AMIP's detectives within twenty-four hours of the meeting in the Corner Pin.

Noel Christopher was, at 25, the youngest. Quiet and shy, he had never been in trouble with the police. Jerome Collins was a few months older than Noel and like his friend had not previously been the subject of police enquiries. John Redai was 28 – he had been in Britain less than a year, but checks with the New Zealand police revealed that he had no criminal record. Alan Peckham, a year younger, was likewise unknown to the Metropolitan Police.

Only Brian Gallagher, five months older than Alan, had a record for a minor offence. All told, the party was stereotypically normal: quiet, decent young men going out on Saturday night to celebrate a friend's birthday in some style.

Alan Peckham later told the police:

> We arrived at the Corner Pin at about 8.45 pm and stayed until about 10.40 pm. At this stage it was just the four of us, John, Noel, Jerome and myself. I think we all bought a round so we had about four drinks.
> Three of us were drinking pints of lager with lemonade top.

I think Noel had one pint and then drank halves. Once we left
the pub we walked to Nelson's. I suppose the walk took
around fifteen minutes and we arrived at the club at about
11.00 pm. It was very quiet, there weren't many people in
there when we got in.

Nelson's nightclub is sited underneath the main
stand at Wimbledon Football Club. On Saturday afternoons it
resounds with the shouts and chants of the crowd above it:
during the evenings it throbs to the pulse of modern dance
music, pumped through an array of powerful loudspeakers.

It boasts, in addition to a small dance-floor and a few
scattered stools, chairs and tables, a late-night drinking
licence which allows its allotted limit of 200 patrons to consume
alcohol until 2.00 am on Sunday mornings.

Beer, wine and spirits do not, in themselves, cause men and
women to kill each other. There is, nonetheless, a link between
the two. The availability of alcohol either acts as a magnet to
draw together those statistically most likely to be murderer
and victim, or as an accelerator – or, frequently, as both
together. And since the sale of alcohol depends for its volume
on the amount of money in people's pockets, the health of a
local economy can have a marked effect on the murder rate.

This is no new theory. From 1876 onwards a series of
European socio-criminological studies showed a positive
relationship between a booming (or at least growing) economy
and crimes of personal violence. This historical analysis was
summed up in 1971 by two German analysts, Radzinowicz and
Wolfgang, in a paper called 'Economic Pressures':

> During periods of prosperity and depression larceny and
> assaults move in converse directions. Crimes against the
> person (such as assault and battery) tend to go up during a
> period of prosperity and often decrease during a depression.
> A similar trend has been observed with respect to sexual
> offences.

The Home Office maintains its own internal research
department to study, amongst other issues, trends within the

commission of crime. During 1989 one of its researchers, Simon Field, was investigating the link between offending and the state of the economy.

He began with a broad database of twelve different categories of crime – from burglary to the use of 'violence against the person' – spread across the years since the end of the Second World War. Within the violent crime category were statistics relating to murder, manslaughter and assaults where the force used could have endangered life.

His brief was deceptively simple: to check whether there was a provable relationship between the wealth of the nation and the types and rates of criminal behaviour.

But although the idea was attractively uncomplicated, it needed a very special type of assessment.

> The analysis of trends in crime, as with any similar data, is a complex technical and theoretical task. To demonstrate a statistical relationship it is not enough to show that two factors show trends in the same direction; this could be pure coincidence.
>
> Instead the revelation of a more subtle interconnection of patterns over time is required. Moreover, in analysing patterns over time, it is also necessary to take into account the possibility that a causal factor will have an impact on crime only after a delay, and the level of crime itself is likely to influence the level of crime at a later date.

To accommodate this need for a sensitive measuring system Field turned to the statistical science of econometrics.

> It has been developed primarily by economists who have a particular interest in changes over time in sets of interwoven economic variables – such as interest rates, exchange rates, unemployment and economic growth. The field of econometrics has developed rapidly over the last two or three decades, and the tools are now readily available with which to tackle statistical time series such as those for recorded crime.

Armed with this responsive analytical tool, Field set about testing the theory that crime and money were inextricably linked other than by the umbilical cords of greed and jealousy.

It should come as no surprise, given the way English law and legal policy developed as an arm of the property protection industry, that the survey first addressed the effects of recession and depression on burglary and related offences.

The results were, perhaps, less than surprising: whenever the economy is weak – and therefore jobs are tight and money short – theft and related offences increase.

> In years when people are increasing their spending very little – or even reducing it – property crime tends to grow relatively quickly, whereas during years when people are rapidly increasing their expenditure property crime tends to grow less rapidly or even fall. In England and Wales the relationship has held throughout the twentieth century and has been particularly strong in the past twenty years.

However politically uncomfortable this notion might be – and the response of some politicians on the right was to dismiss the finding as dangerous nonsense – the logic behind it is relatively easily absorbed: deprivation coupled with envy is one side of an equation whose ultimate solution is frequently theft.

But it was when Field turned his attention to personal crimes of violence that he unearthed a truly revealing statistical analysis of the effects of the economic cycle.

> Personal crime – sexual offences and violence against the person (but not robbery) – also shows a distinctive relation to personal consumption. It appears to increase in line with consumption, so that personal crime appears to increase more rapidly during periods of rapidly increasing consumption.
>
> This means that personal crime responds to consumption growth in the *opposite* manner to that of property crime: during periods of slow consumption growth, personal crime tends to grow more slowly than usual, whereas in periods of rapid consumption growth, personal crime tends to grow more rapidly.

Field turned particular attention to the patterns of crime

and growth throughout the 1980s: they matched exactly the patterns he had analysed across the four decades of his study, and reflected the boom-bust economy of the Thatcher years with such precision that the implication was inescapable.

> The most striking feature of these trends has been the way in which during the first years of the decade in 1980 and 1981, recorded property crime of most types grew very rapidly, while personal crime grew very little.
> There followed a gradual reversal in this pattern, such that personal crime grew rapidly in 1987 and 1988, while property crime grew very little during the same period. This shift can now be attributed at least in part to the business cycle: personal consumption actually fell during the 1980–1 recession – so that a high rate of property crime growth and a low rate of personal crime growth might have been expected.
> Consumption grew extremely fast in 1987–8, underlying the observed reverse pattern of low (or negative) property crime growth and rapid growth in personal crime.

Next Field decided to analyse what it was about boom years in the economy which appeared to promote – or at least reflect – an increase in violent crime.

> Personal crime in the form of violence against the person and sexual offences responds positively to rapid consumption growth. Personal crime is not directly affected by the goods available to the victim or the offender, but is affected by the pattern of routine activities, which in turn is affected by consumption and income growth.
> There is good evidence that people who go out more often are much more likely to be the victims of personal crime than those who do not, and there is also evidence that when consumption increases some of that consumption goes on increased time spent outside the home.
> This suggests an explanation for the observed positive relation between personal crime and consumption: when spending rises people spend more time outside the home, and as a result there are more opportunities for personal crime.

If this applied to personal crime as a generic problem, it has a particular relevance to the statistics which show that, of murder victims, young men are the single most likely group. Spending time outside the home is, as Field was to deduce, often a euphemistic way of describing long nights in pubs, clubs and discos. So the equation was becoming clearer.

Give young men, in particular, the wherewithal to go out for a good time, and immediately the prospect of an increased attendance at the most likely location for conflict is increased.

In part, of course, this is due to the effect of alcohol. Field studied the effect of alcohol consumption across the decades on crime against property and against the person. In the latter category he arrived at an interesting statistical discovery.

> Violence against the person was found to be strongly related to the level of beer consumption – although not to other forms of alcohol consumption or with the number of on- and off-licences.
>
> The implication of this finding is: while alcohol as such is not a cause of violence against the person, a particular combination of alcohol and social circumstances – perhaps young men drinking a lot of beer in pubs and clubs – is conducive to crime of this type.

Intrigued, the researcher next examined the statistical pattern of beer consumption: it matched with uncanny precision the pattern of crimes of violence in the decades from the mid-1950s onward.

At which point it would be relatively easy to dismiss Field's findings as having little importance for the development of criminal justice policy: after all, young men have been drinking beer, fighting and frequently causing each other's death since ale was invented. Why, other than as a reaction to an overall 9 per cent growth over four decades, should we pay the figures any undue attention?

The answer lies in one last, and revealing, piece of statistical evidence which Field uncovered. Not merely did murder and other forms of violent attack mirror the erratic swings of the Thatcher-era economy, but they had a particular relationship with unemployment.

Field's study had shown that, whatever the economy –

property crime axis, there was no convincing evidence to link burglary and other theft offences with unemployment. But murder, violent assault and sex crime were different:

> Growth in offences of violence against the person was also found to be associated with growth in unemployment during the previous year. This was the only type of crime found to be connected with unemployment, and the relation is strong.
> These results strongly suggest that unemployment, and the relative deprivation associated with it, are conducive to violent crime.

If at first this seems paradoxical, at odds with the evidence of a link between economical growth and violence, Field was able to supply potential explanations.

> It has been argued that consumption growth induces changes in lifestyle which increase the risk of personal crime; these may be the violent crimes of affluence, connected with pubs, clubs and places of entertainment. Conversely there may be violent crimes of poverty related in part to the frustration and poverty of unemployment. Domestic violence may fall into this category.

The physical abuse of women and children in the home may or may not be explained by unemployment: the statistics which indicate a rise in such offences are unreliable because there has been – at long last – a greater willingness on behalf of police to investigate them, and a corresponding rise in the confidence of abused women to report them.

But the violent crimes of affluence suffer from no such statistical problems. The fact is that the 1980s was the decade of 'designer violence': football hooligans carrying Stanley knives to carve up their rivals' faces most typically wore expensive Pringle sweaters and enjoyed the luxury of well-paid jobs in banks and commerce.

Rural violence involving not the long-term unemployed but those new on the employment ladder became a feature of the boom years. Field's statistical analysis underlined the fact that those whom the press came to dub 'lager louts' with cash in their pockets, had previously been unemployed in the bankrupt years of the Thatcher economy. The message was simple: create an underclass of deprived, disaffected youth and then thrust upon it the heady benefits of an economy booming out of control, and a Caliban creature will result – violent, callous and drunken.

If ever three young men epitomised this stereotype of eighties man, it was the group which strutted in to Nelson's nightclub at 11.45 pm on Saturday, 30 December.

Brett Simon White was 23 – though he looked much older – five feet nine inches tall, with a lean muscular body and short brown hair. His clothes were expensive and fashionable, in the style of South London suburbia.

Adrian Dennis Williams was twelve years older and a good deal heavier. The smartness of his neatly trimmed beard, short hair and mid-grey suit was belied by an impressive gallery of tattoos stretching from his fingers up the greater part of both his muscular arms.

Gary Robert Bateson was 25, slim but muscular and, like his friends, wore fashionably tailored hair and neat – if rather gaudy – clothes.

Brett White worked as a trainee manager at the Cricketers, a pub in Sutton with a reputation for a degree of unwelcome violence and a clientèle, many of whom had some acquaintance with the workings of the criminal justice system.

By the age of 23 he had acquired a wife and a 2-year-old child, swiftly followed by a separation and a pending divorce. Details of his own childhood are minimal, but as a youth he belonged to two amateur boxing clubs and fought at least twelve formal bouts. He won each time.

Whether or not this played a part in his other extra-curricular activities is open to speculation. Certainly he was known to be handy with his fists: he had accumulated five convictions, three of them for causing actual bodily harm to those he encountered in pubs or clubs. His last conviction for assault had occurred after he punched and kicked a complete stranger at a disco in the Surrey town of Redhill. The victim's 'crime' was to wish White's then fiancée a Merry Christmas.

In the middle of May 1989 he had met a young bank clerk called Susan Stevens. She was 18 years old and drinking often at the Cricketers when White began using the pub as a regular haunt.

> On 29 July Brett surprised me with a ring and we became engaged. In December Brett became the trainee manager at the Cricketers, and took over the flat above the pub. I moved in with him two weeks later. I slept there every night, but went home for food and washing. On 2 December I began working as a barmaid at the Cricketers, too.

On the Saturday in question, the couple started work behind the bar at 7.30 pm. An hour later Adrian Williams arrived. By 10.30 pm Gary Bateson and his girlfriend, Sally Partridge, had joined them.

It is, perhaps, significant – given the picture of violent crime to be drawn from Simon Field's Home Office survey – that of the five young men and women who would subsequently leave the Cricketers together and head for Nelson's nightclub, only Susan Stevens was without a criminal record.

Gary Bateson had known Brett White since they were 11 years old. Both men looked on each other as *de facto* 'brothers', to the point where they had been involved in many of the same fights. In addition, White had married, and later divorced, Bateson's sister. According to Detective Inspector David Cooper:

> Bateson had four previous convictions, including two for using threatening behaviour. His last conviction was for assault causing actual bodily harm and it followed an incident in a pub when he punched a man who was apparently making comments about him.
> In February 1989 he was arrested with Brett White after an allegation of assault at a disco in Purley, Surrey. Both men were released by local police and after that it appears that

witnesses were influenced as no charges were preferred. As a
youth he, like White, belonged to amateur boxing clubs.

Adrian Williams, known to his friends as 'Ady', had amassed
an impressive tally of fifteen previous convictions, including
threatening behaviour, actual bodily harm and unlawful
wounding. Of the three he bore the most evidently threatening
pose and appearance of the traditional pub lout.

The three men and two young women decided to go for a late
drink at Nelson's and when White and Susan Stevens finished
work, all five climbed into her father's red Nissan hatchback
for the short drive across town. They arrived at 11.45 pm and
took up a position near the bar, overlooking the dance-floor. A
few yards away, Noel Christopher and his friends were
enjoying their night out.

Nelson's, unlike many similar nightclubs, did not have a
reputation for trouble. A well-run club, according to local
police, it boasted business-like bouncers on the door who were
available to break up fights on the rare occasions when they
started.

The club itself was on two levels. The bar and some seating
was on one level, separated from the dance-floor by a low
wooden partition. Other seats and tables lay further into the
room on a slightly raised dais.

Alan Peckham was the first to notice the group which
stationed itself across the carpeted floor alongside the wooden
divider. At first he, and Brian Gallagher who had joined Noel's
party at the club, saw only one young blonde woman: White,
Bateson and Williams had gone to buy the first round of drinks;
Sally Partridge was in the toilet.

In the way of most young single men out for a Saturday night
on the town, Brian Gallagher first appraised the woman's
looks, then the chances of her being free.

After an initial glance he turned to Noel Christopher and
said: 'Not bad, but she has to be with someone.' A few minutes
later he looked over again and saw three muscular men join the
women and pass over a selection of drinks. 'Told you,' he
commented to Noel, 'she had to be with someone.'

John Redai wandered away shortly afterwards to dance with a girl he had met at the bar. Noel's group of friends – Alan Peckham, Jerome Collins and Brian Gallagher – continued talking and drinking. Occasionally one or other of them would look across the room at the party on the other side of the room.

Just after 1.00 am Gary Bateson walked across to Alan Peckham and stood directly in front of him. He put both muscular arms on the young man's shoulders and said: 'Is everything all right?'

On a scale of overtly threatening remarks, 'Is everything all right' might not appear unduly aggressive. But it was the way Gary Bateson uttered the words that worried Alan Peckham – they were clearly not intended to convey any concern for his welfare.

Susan Stevens had been aware of the young men appraising her from across the room, but the attention had not unduly worried her. But Brett White and his friends were a different matter: they took immense exception to anyone staring – or even looking – at them or their girlfriends. Susan Stevens recalled:

> There was talk amongst Gary, Brett and Ady that some blokes kept staring at them. I can't remember the actual words, but they were getting wound up.
>
> From what I know of Brett, Ade and Gary, none of them like being stared at. A common expression would be something like 'He's screwing me out'. Gary had been stared at in the Cricketers a couple of times. I have seen him go over to other men and speak to them when he has been stared at.
>
> On the night at Nelson's they were all getting very wound up by the group staring. At some moment things changed, though I cannot describe how. I suppose I knew that something was going to be said – I mean that they were going to front them out. I just knew it was going to happen, either then or outside somewhere. Gary, Brett and Ady are not the type of men to take being stared at. I knew it was not going to be ignored.

Alan Peckham considered Gary Bateson's question: it did not seem to make much sense. He decided to ignore it, and turned back to Noel Christopher and his own group of friends. It was his turn to buy the round. Before he had opened his mouth to ask who wanted a drink, a glass was smashed on the back of his head, dousing him in beer. He fell down.

Jerome Collins had leaned forward to hear what Gary Bateson was saying to Alan Peckham. Without warning he felt a hard punch drive into his cheek bone. The force of the blow spun him round and sideways, but he managed to stay upright. Brian Gallagher caught a simultaneous punch on his face from another fist and fell down dazed.

From that moment on it was open season on Noel Christopher's group: White, Bateson and Williams were experienced pub brawlers. Fists flew from all directions: the only thing certain to those around them was that the tough looking threesome were getting the better of the exchange.

Stuart Davey was a driver by day and doorman by night. He and his colleagues at Nelson's took it in turns to stand at the door turning away undesirable revellers, and to circulate amongst those who had been allowed in.

I was standing beside the disc jockey, beside the dance-floor, when I became aware of the disturbance. It seemed there was a group of six or seven people confronting each other. I ran over across the dance-floor and started to pull people back to enable me to get to the heart of the problem.

By the time I arrived at the group, if there had been fighting it had finished, and the group were just shouting abuse at each other.

I remember putting two men in headlocks under my arms when I heard shouting and a challenging chant from behind me. I turned to my right and saw a man walk straight across to face a young boy and without hesitation he made a punching movement with his right hand straight into the stomach of the boy, who doubled up under the force of the blow, then slumped to the floor.

The man backed away slightly, stuffing something into his right-hand trouser pocket; he seemed to be having a problem with whatever it was. I presumed it was a knife.

I let go of the two men I was holding and looked straight at the man. I could see the other doorman going towards him,

and I moved towards him as well. I heard the man shout 'You
want some as well then, mate!' I glanced across to the floor
and could see the young boy was bleeding from a stomach
wound. I shouted a warning to the other doorman: 'Watch out,
he's tooled up'.

As Stuart Davey and the second doorman moved towards the
man with the knife, Noel Christopher – the gentle man who
looked more like a boy and loved animals – lay very still on the
floor, holding his hand across his stomach. Alan Peckham
moved his hand and saw a spreading red stain. He began
talking to Noel, reassuring him that the wound was no more
than a graze, saying anything in the vague realisation that he
needed to keep his friend conscious. Noel lay still: he nodded
once and said 'Yeah'. That was all.

Susan Stevens watched the brawl from across the room. It
was not an unfamiliar sight: in the short time she had been
going out with Brett White it had become apparent that he was
not a man reluctant to use his fists.

It was a short fight. I saw each of them – Brett, Gary and Ady
– punch at the men who were staring at them. It was all over
so quickly there could only have been a few punches.
    From what I know of them they went over to pick a fight. I
cannot imagine them going over and asking them to stop
staring – it just wouldn't happen like that. They were to
blame for going over to the other group of men . . . they went
over for a fight.
    It was inevitable as no one stares at people like them and
gets away with it. They can handle themselves when things
get rough. Gary can get fairly 'lairy' [argumentative and
violent], especially when he is drunk. In fact he is always like
this.

There is a note of desperation in these statements: Susan
Stevens had been due to marry Brett White in a little under a
year. As she described what she saw, she knew the wedding
was to be postponed indefinitely.

Her fiancé had been the man Stuart Davey saw with the
knife – the knife which he had punched once, brutally, into
Noel Christopher's stomach.

Even then Brett White was far from finished. Nathaniel Jacobs, known to his friends and colleagues as 'Cliff', was the other doorman on duty that night. As Davey turned to face White, Nathaniel ran full tilt towards the *mêlée*.

> I could see the injured man lying against the low wall with blood by the side of his mouth. I was aware of one particular man who walked round everybody else and went across to a man I assume was a friend of the injured man. He started abusing him, grabbing him by the shoulders.
>
> I heard him say to the other man, 'If you want it you'll get it'. I stood between them to separate them, trying to calm him down. He said, 'If you want it you can get it instead.' He then put his face right up close to mine and we were having an eyeball confrontation. He said, 'Come on outside'.
>
> I immediately grabbed him and pinned him against the wall with my left hand and punched him three or four times at least in the face with my right hand. I had been looking at the injured man and it was obvious he had been stabbed: I didn't want to give him any chance to stab me.
>
> After I punched him I kept hold of him. As he fell to the floor I was leaning over him holding him down when I felt my hair being pulled from behind. Someone also pulled my leg and the man slipped away.
>
> He went over to a table and smashed a glass on the edge. He then held the broken glass in front of him threatening me and beckoning me towards him with the other hand. Mark William Harris [another bouncer] went across and tried to pacify him, but as he did I saw a second man aged about 35 years old with a full beard and a double-breasted suit waving a knife about in his left hand and I heard him say, 'I'm going to get a shotgun and do you.'

As Ady Williams engineered a stand-off, Brett White dropped the glass and with Gary Bateson looked around for their girlfriends.

Susan Stevens had turned her back on the brawl some minutes earlier, calmly walking over to the counter where she had handed in her coat more than an hour before. She snapped at the girl behind the desk, 'I want my coat now,' thrusting the ticket in her face.

> All I was concerned with at the time was what was happening with Brett. I didn't pay any attention to anybody else. I didn't see anybody with a knife and the bouncers told us to leave the club.

It would be appealing to believe Susan Stevens when she denies knowing about a knife. But even if the evidence of Ady Williams waving his knife about at anyone within range could be discounted, the doormen that night recall a telling conversation as the group pushed their way out of the exit.

Richard Tucker was the most senior of the bouncers at Nelson's that night. He had seen Brett White and Gary Bateson in the club on several previous occasions, but he believed – as did many of their own friends – that the men were brothers.

> The bloke on the floor was moaning and Mark, one of the doormen, was putting an ice-pack on his stomach. I could see the bloke's clothing and he looked serious. I went over to the taller brother [White] who was standing with Nathaniel to the left of the entrance stairway.
>
> I went up to the taller brother and said, 'What's going on here: have you stabbed him or what?' He said, 'No, I've had a straightener with the geezer: I don't use knives.' I said, 'Have you stabbed him or not?' He said, 'No.' The two girls came over to where I was and the girl in white [Stevens] said, 'Come on, let's go: I've had enough of this.'
>
> I was now aware the other brother and the [man in the] grey suit were just to my right. Both the brothers said almost together, 'No, we're going to stay and sort it all out.' I then went back over to see how the bloke on the floor was. I looked back towards the entrance a minute later and saw the group of five had gone.

White, Bateson and Williams had decided to get out before the police arrived. Before slipping through the main door, Brett White handed Sally Partridge a red-handled, thin-bladed lock-knife: she hid it underneath her arm as they walked out into the night.

As they reached the car park a posse of four uniformed police constables walked past them and into the chaos of the

nightclub. Sally Partridge asked Bateson what she should do
with White's knife. He told her to throw it as far away as she
could. When she did not – could not – do it, he took it from her
and hurled it up on the grass bank at the Wandle Terrace end of
the football ground. Williams dropped his own, dark-green-
handled flick-knife in the undergrowth nearby.

If Brett White was shocked by what he knew he had done, it
did not show. He talked through the fight with his brawling
partners before setting off in search of a late-night snack.
According to Susan Stevens who drove them that night:

> On the way from the club in the car Brett, Gary and Ady said
> they [Noel Christopher and his friends] deserved being hit
> because they had been staring and winding them up all night.
> Then Brett, Gary and Ady went into the kebab house
> together, and we all went back to the Cricketers.

Noel Christopher, meanwhile, was being gingerly lifted on to
a stretcher and carried out to a police ambulance: there was, at
the time, an ambulance strike in London, and the Metropolitan
Police was having to provide auxiliary drivers.

Had Noel been able to overhear the conversation in Susan
Stevens' car it might, at least, have answered the one question
he managed to ask: 'Why me?'

He died at 8.00 that morning, his father by the bedside. Noel
Christopher had been unlucky. Brett White had stabbed him
only once, but the three-quarter-inch fish-tailed wound was at
a point directly over his upper abdomen. The blade had pierced
the abdominal wall before transfixing the colon and breaking
into the neck of the pancreas. Superintendent Bill Lavers, the
SIO who would take on the case:

> Surgeons these days can do wonders. We call it the East
> Belfast effect: because of the troubles in that part of Northern
> Ireland, doctors have become adept at sewing people back
> together.
>   But there are places in the body which are soft and
> vulnerable and it takes only one unlucky wound to kill you.
> That's what happened to Noel Christopher: he

haemorrhaged to death because the knife cut through so many vital organs.

There had been around 130 people in Nelson's that night. When Bill Lavers was called out to the scene many – perhaps most – had already slipped away. Only those who had been close to the action and had witnessed the stabbing and subsequent fracas were available to give the detective his first hints of how to progress with the investigation.

One of his first appointments was the key figure of his second in command. He chose a local divisional inspector with some experience of major incident work. David Cooper had been a detective sergeant in 4 AMIP a few years previously: he had during one celebrated investigation worked as Bob Chapman's dedicated 'bagman'. He at least would know the ropes.

Lavers assessed the situation. It was the early hours of New Year's Eve. He had witnesses to three men and two women, together as a group, who appeared to have come into the nightclub just before midnight and within an hour become involved in what seemed likely to be recorded as a fatal fight.

None of the eye-witnesses could name the people in the group, and most of the other revellers had gone. Above all, in less than twelve hours all of London would start to party again – and in a big way. The end of the decade was at hand, and it was not about to let Lavers' investigation get in the way. It was not, he reflected, a particularly promising start.

The only reasonable lead he could get to work on was a set of remarkably consistent descriptions of the three men by those who had been closest to them.

Eyewitnesses can be a real disadvantage. It's not that they tell you lies or deliberately mislead you, it's just that they think they saw things they actually didn't. You have to exercise a good deal of caution, otherwise you can end up the garden path following a lead which turns out to be completely wrong.

Among the descriptions was Richard Tucker's statement that he knew two of the men to be brothers. It could have proved disastrous. Brett White and Gary Bateson were indeed related – but they were brothers-in-law rather than blood brothers. Had Lavers actively sought out genuine siblings he might well have lost valuable time in the crucial first seventy-two hours of his enquiry.

But Richard Tucker did have one small piece of valuable information. One of the men, he was able to tell Lavers, not one of the brothers but the bearded man with them, was known as 'Ady'. It was not a lot to go on but it was about all the SIO had.

As the AMIP swung into action, taking photographs, supervising forensic scene-of-crime tests, logging crime scene materials, setting up an incident room and beginning the dreary task of taking statements, Brett White and Susan Stevens were in bed. So too was Noel Christopher. The difference was that he was dead.

Throughout that Sunday morning the detectives followed through the established pattern of the beginnings of a major incident enquiry. Lavers assigned officers to check whether those witnesses who had been interviewed had criminal records – and therefore might not necessarily be telling the truth – others to liaising with Noel's family and yet more to searching the area outside the club for any potential evidence.

At 12.41 pm the first of that evidence was found. Police Constable Graham Kite was quartering the grass embankment at the back of Wandle Terrace. Kite was a uniformed officer and trained dog handler: with him that afternoon was his police dog, Kerri.

As Kerri sniffed and searched through the undergrowth, she suddenly stopped: Kite looked over. In the long grass beneath her snout he saw a green-handled flick-knife.

Lavers, as with all AMIP SIOs facing a new murder enquiry, had pulled together a team of detectives at short notice from all across the Division. Creating a new and labour-intensive pool such as this in such short order is never a particularly easy task: on New Year's Eve it was complicated further by the natural desire of many officers to be home with their families.

At first glance this might seem to be a shortcoming of the

AMIP system: forcing experienced leaders like Bill Lavers to
rely, at the moment of most severe pressure, on an assortment
of detectives from stations throughout the Division with little
or no knowledge of their level of training and expertise.

But it can also be a strength. Murder is predominantly a local
affair, committed by men and women in, around or near their
home territory. The presence on an investigation of officers
with a local copper's basic knowledge can prove invaluable. As
day one of the enquiry into the death of Noel Christopher drew
to a close, Bill Lavers was to see this truth in action.

Like his colleagues, Lavers knows the importance of the
office meeting – that free-for-all where ideas are kicked around
no matter how junior their source, how remote their likelihood
of progress. On Sunday, 31 December 1989, he called the
newly-assembled team together in the hastily-created
incident room at Wimbledon police station.

Each officer summarised the information he or she had
received. New facts, opinions, suspicions were aired in front of
all the team for the first time. It was in this way that the vague
identification of a violent man with a short-cropped beard,
accompanying the two 'brothers' and generally pitching into
the fight was discussed. The only clue to his identity – that he
appeared to be known as 'Ady' – was explained to the room at
large. Inspector David Cooper recalls:

> It was then that one of the local lads we had drafted in said
> that he knew – in fact he had arrested – an 'Ady' who
> matched the physical description, and whose criminal record
> seemed to fit the behaviour of the man in the club. This 'Ady'
> was called Adrian Williams, and the officer thought he lived
> at a pub in Sutton called the Cricketers.

It might seem a slim lead – it probably was. But it was all the
AMIP had to go on. Lavers faced an instant decision: should he
go to the pub on New Year's Eve when it would be full and
lively? Or should he leave it overnight and attempt to pick up
the man in the morning?

The decision was made more critical by local knowledge of

the Cricketers. It was not, apparently, a pub known for the quality of its clientèle. There was a very real danger – particularly given the date and the time – that an indiscreet entry by a number of detectives and uniformed police might start a small-scale riot.

Lavers decided to go to the pub in an unmarked car, but ordered back-up support from local stations to be ready if needed. He had also formulated a plan of action in his own mind: rather than march in mob-handed, he would summon the landlord out to him.

At 9.00 pm, a car containing Lavers, his bagman and David Cooper pulled up outside the pub. The landlord was sent for and brought back to the car.

> We began asking him about a man called Adrian Williams. At first he wasn't too cooperative. He said he knew him but he hadn't seen him that night. We agreed that he would take us through the pub and identify Williams if we saw him.
>
> We went through fairly carefully, through the bar, in the back, in the kitchen. But there was no sign of our man. Out at the back of the pub I found a set of steps up to what looked like some sort of flat. I asked the landlord what was up there, but he said there was nothing – just a storeroom and it was locked. He didn't know where the key was.

Lavers and Cooper offered the landlord an instant decision: find the key – and quickly – or the AMIP would break down the door. The key was found.

Then, with the landlord and supporting officers, they gingerly climbed the stairs and opened the door.

> But what I saw wasn't one bloke with a beard. There were two men there: I hadn't actually expected that. I identified myself and asked which one was Adrian Williams. The older of the two said he was. I then told him I was arresting him on suspicion of being involved in the fight in the pub, and I turned to the other man. I looked at him and realised he fitted the description of the taller 'brother': it was a bit of a gamble, but I arrested him as well.

Though David Cooper did not know it, he had just arrested Brett White, a man who objected to being looked at, former owner of a red-handled lock-knife, an experienced brawler – and killer of Noel Christopher.

Beneath the veneer of most self-proclaimed 'hard men' there lurks the embarrassed reality of a little boy. It is this combination of power and vulnerability which, according to some women, makes bullies irresistible. But it also makes for a sad and pathetic spectacle. Brett White and Ady Williams surrendered meekly to David Cooper and allowed themselves to be led down the narrow stairs with barely a murmur. It was, perhaps, just as well. In the confusion of the moment Cooper found he had arrived in the flat uncomfortably far ahead of his colleagues. 'It could have turned nasty – and I'd have been there on my own for a couple of minutes. Fortunately both men came quietly.'

Neither White nor Williams knew at that stage that Noel Christopher was dead. To them the fracas at Nelson's had been only marginally out of the run of their normal aggressive behaviour. That margin of difference was provided by the red-handled lock-knife and a three-quarter-inch wound in Noel's abdomen.

The men were bundled into Lavers's unmarked car and driven across suburbia to Wimbledon police station. Because it was New Year's Eve, and because of the unexpected arrests, Lavers and Cooper faced an immediate logistical problem. The Police and Criminal Evidence Act (PACE) dictated that if he wanted to interview the suspects he had to do so on audio tape. To this end most police stations big enough to be used by an AMIP team now have tailor-made recording facilities – a dual cassette system screwed securely to the table. Suspects are given one copy of the tape, the detectives retain the other.

But at Wimbledon that night there was no dedicated interview room available. The detectives faced a difficult choice: hold the men until one could be found, or attempt a Heath Robinson recording with whatever they could find in the cupboards and lockers around the station.

It was PACE which swayed them. Although the Act allows police to detain a suspect for twenty-four hours – thirty-six on the authority of a superintendent or higher ranking officer – it requires six-hourly reviews throughout that period.

At those junctures a decision must be reached by the station inspector and relying only on known and firm evidence whether to continue holding the suspect. Lavers and Cooper had little choice: if they delayed until a full recording room was available they might exceed the six-hour limit with nothing to show. They dug out a 'ghetto blaster' personal tape recorder and began the first of a series of interviews.

Both White and Williams were interviewed separately; both admitted being in Nelson's the previous evening. Williams admitted throwing one solitary punch, but denied having a flick-knife.

Brett White steadfastly denied any involvement in the brawl. He did so throughout two long interviews. But Ady Williams put him in the frame; Sally Partridge had been arrested and was talking too. Lavers decided to have White moved across to South Norwood police station where there were full recording facilities. He also agreed to allow him access to his solicitor.

What passed between the lawyer and White during those long hours of 1 January 1990 remains confidential. But the outcome was dramatic. Brett White summoned the detectives back to the interview room with the message that he wanted to make a third statement.

In the bare, unforgiving room, across a battered wooden desk and in the presence of White's solicitor, the AMIP team formally cautioned their suspect and waited for him to open the proceedings.

> Um, the last two interviews have not all been true . . . um . . . yes, unfortunately I did have a knife and yes unfortunately I did stab the young man that died on Saturday night with a knife . . .
>
>   Believe it or not it's the first time I've ever taken a knife out with me . . . um . . . the reason I had the knife was I used to

have a greengrocer's shop at Rose Hill and that was one of the
knives I used to use for doing all my trimming up with . . . um
. . . why I particularly took it out that night I don't know.

With hindsight it was not a convincing explanation: most
greengrocers do not use fancy red lock-knives to trim the ends
from their produce. Relatively few are caught taking such
weapons to nightclubs. Rarely is one charged with murder as a
result.

White's answers to the detectives' insistent probing begin as
attempts to minimise his actions or place the blame for the
fracas on Noel Christopher and his friends. In this, at least,
they are typical early statements from unreconstructed
offenders, that is those still refusing to accept the reality of
their crime. As more information came to light – whether from
Williams or Partridge – it was put to White: his story altered to
accommodate it.

Thus at first he claimed he had dropped his knife in the club
itself. Then Sally Partridge's allegation that he had asked her
to carry it out and dispose of it was put to him. Grudgingly he
accepted the accusation.

In between the justification and minimisations lies the third
component of offenders' statements the world over: self-pity
and egotism:

I dunno why [I stabbed Noel]. I suppose it was on the moment,
panic. I mean there's no way I would ever want to kill
somebody. Maybe temporarily hurt them. Not kill them, or
murder them . . .
First time I've ever took a knife out as well. Never, ever
took anything out with me. First time I've ever done that and
it's fucking done this . . .
I dunno, I just can't believe that I've done that to somebody
because I've, I've . . . well anyone who knows me, I'll fight
anyone . . . I am that person. And well I haven't been beaten
yet, so why I should use that I don't know.
I'm so disgusted . . . I'm just so – well, how do you feel after
you know you've stabbed somebody and killed them? Just feel
numb, just feel nothing, feel so fucking stupid, because I
know I can do whatever I want with my hands and feet and

the head. Why I should ever have took that out and used it I
don't know.

But Brett White admitted he had used the red lock-knife;
that he had driven it into Noel Christopher's belly – just once,
but that had been enough to kill him. And he admitted he knew
he had made contact: the talk in the car as the youths and their
girls sped away from Nelson's had revolved around the
evening's 'entertainment'.

There was little to entertain Noel's family. Murder is always
traumatic for those left behind to pick up its pieces. Suddenly
and without warning they are thrust into the confusion of an
alien world of police and court procedures. Even the victim's
body is not under their control: to bury or cremate it requires
the agreement of the court.

Throughout the early hours of the Sunday morning Noel's
sister Gloria had sat in the accident and emergency department of St Georges's Hospital, Tooting. Beside her was her
father. In the theatre across the way, surgeons had fought to
save Noel's life. At 7.15 that New Year's Eve morning he had a
massive heart attack. By 8.00 am he had died.

> Suddenly I began to scream with shock and pain, while my
> father sat there quietly sobbing by my side. The hospital staff
> were very kind but there was little they could do to ease our
> dreadful feelings of loss and disbelief.
>
> Then I drove my father through the streets, full of people
> welcoming in the New Year, to a friend's house where we
> both collapsed in tears, barely able to explain what we'd been
> through.
>
> We spent most of that day going over what had happened
> and trying to make sense of it. Who had done this to Noel and
> for God's sake why?
>
> The next few months were a nightmare. We were not
> allowed to have Noel's body back for eight weeks because of
> the murder enquiry. We were then advised not to bury him
> because if there was an appeal the defence could ask to have
> Noel's body exhumed for up to five years after the case. None
> of the family could face this idea so we finally decided to have
> him cremated.

There is an organisation which attempts to help those who suffer from the trauma of serious crime. The National Victims' Support Scheme works throughout Britain with the families of homicide victims in particular. Every year their staff see the grieving parents or children, sisters and brothers of the victims of up to 600 separate killings.

There is a syndrome that these workers have noticed, too. As murder in pub brawls becomes an increasingly common way of death for young men, society becomes less supportive, less understanding of the victim's relatives. The reasoning appears to be one of levels of innocence. So, compared to death at the hands of a brutal burglar or abusive partner, the killing of a youth in the street seems to be viewed as somehow his fault. The stigma is particularly great for victims killed in increasingly violent streets, pubs and clubs.

Noel Christopher's family should not, in a rational world, have had to face any such callousness: Noel was no lout about town deserving of a pointless and painful death in public. But the taint remained.

Gloria decided she needed to find out who it was who had turned the family's world upside down.

> We had been told shortly after Noel's death that several youths had been charged, but it was only after the funeral that I had time to start wondering who they were, and try to put a face to the names I had been told about. I began to find myself looking at young men in the street thinking to myself, could it be you that killed my brother?

In fact the murderer was in the remand wing of Brixton Prison. Brett White had appeared in court – briefly – on Tuesday, 2 January 1990. He was remanded in custody for nine months.

> It was very tough being locked up for the first time, but I knew I deserved no better. At least it gave me time to start taking in what I had actually done. The more I thought about Noel, the more I hated myself.
>
> When I appeared in court I appeared to show no emotion, but I was behaving as I had been advised. It went totally

against my nature to stand there listening to what I had done without showing my real feelings.

Whatever people may think of me, I'm not a monster. How could I be in the same room as the family of a boy I had killed, with my father looking on, and not feel dreadful.

Brett White wrote those words from prison in June 1991. If they sound the words of a temperate man, a reformed and wiser man, we should remember that in prison offenders have time to think. Sometimes they use it to stare into themselves and emerge genuinely changed; sometimes they use it to create a new image for themselves to fool the parole board when the possibility of release appears close. These men conform to a simplistic pattern. They behave wildly immediately on entering the system, and claim a subsequent period of good behaviour as evidence of a reformed character.

Which Brett White are we to believe in? The newly sensitised repentant, or the laddish braggart and bully? Gloria has no such uncertainty. She remembers the words White spat out at her as his mandatory life sentence was imposed: 'Have you got what you wanted now?'

For the record, only Brett White was convicted of the murder of Noel Christopher. Ady Williams was convicted of violent disorder contrary to the 1986 Public Order Act. Gary Bateson was acquitted on all counts. Stevens and Partridge were not charged.

Three young violent men, the product of a decade which saw greed triumph over need, callousness over compassion. As the 1980s drew to their close, Granada Television commissioned a survey of the experiences of young people in Britain. It showed that nearly one in seven men between the danger ages of 16 and 24 reported being attacked in the street. The figure was twelve times higher than that for women.

Inspector David Cooper pushes his glasses up from the bridge of his nose and rubs his eyes. A young detective, still in his thirties, Cooper has dealt with more deaths than most people would see throughout several lifetimes – all carried out by amateurs, all of it unnecessary.

We are becoming a more violent society. I don't think there can be any doubt about that. More people carry knives, more people are prepared to use them.

In the past few weeks I've been called to two cases first where caustic soda was poured over someone's genitals, and then when a mixture of hot chip fat and bleach was thrown in the victim's face.

We call some of this domestic crime. But it can still be murder.

7
The Missing Mandarin

DAVID NAPIER HAMILTON of Brixton:
missing since 19 November 1985. Will
anyone able to give information as to his
whereabouts, health or death please
telephone his brother . . .

Advert in The Times, *November 1986*

County Hall, London, Sunday, 17 November 1985

Dr David Hamilton smiled and firmly shook the hand of the Gambian Minister for Education, before taking his seat at top table. Around him were senior politicians, bureaucrats and diplomats, all assembled for a formal reception and banquet.

Hamilton's job, as it had been for fifteen years, was to ensure that the evening ran smoothly. It was a job he accomplished with natural ease and evident enjoyment. As Head of Protocol in the office of the Chairman of the Greater London Council, he was well used to mixing with government ministers and royalty from across the globe. He was, in his deliberate, quiet way, the very essence of a modern mandarin.

Twenty-four hours later he vanished.

Chief Superintendent Bob Chapman eases back his chair at his favourite golf club in Croydon's semi-rural outskirts, lights a Rothman's Kingsize – *the* brand of police middle management – and smiles in anticipation. It is a good story: a classic whodunnit, a yarn to tell his grandchildren.

> There are some cases which are once in a lifetime jobs – cases where everything combines to test your skills as a detective. If you solve them you can feel satisfied that you've done a damn good job, and there won't be another one like it however long you stay in the job. The David Hamilton investigation was one of those.

Chapman is an amiable man to lunch with – burly, quiet and smart in that very understated way of senior London police-men. Now aged 51, he joined the Metropolitan Police as a uniformed police constable in Brixton before being accepted into CID as a trainee detective in the run-down area of Catford. His first full appointment as a plain-clothes investigator took him to the West End in the days when it was still run by, and on behalf of, indigenous organised crime.

Promotion to sergeant switched him from the glamour of fashionable London to a very different world – Peckham in South London, and a posting to the Flying Squad, the élite and routinely armed investigative unit which tackles major league crime in London.

It was a short hop from 'the Sweeney' [in cockney rhyming slang the Flying Squad is called 'Sweeney Todd'] to working out of Brixton as a detective inspector in the robbery squad.

After a brief detour to the more salubrious surroundings of Kensington – and elevation to detective chief inspector with it – Chapman returned to the Flying Squad to join a team of top detectives investigating the £6 million Security Express robbery in 1983, then Britain's biggest.

In 1985 he was made up to superintendent, thus joining the next tier of police management. A new posting took him further away from the geographic centre of London and symbolically away from the heart of hands-on investigating: Chapman was put in charge of the Force Intelligence Bureau at East Dulwich.

The very existence of the FIB is a reflection of the problems of internal rivalry that dog the Metropolitan Police (an issue we will consider in the next chapter). Ostensibly, the main intelligence division is C11: its staff assemble raw data on major criminals and syndicates – either international or domestic – and supply the refined information they process to New Scotland Yard.

In theory, the Yard also acts as a conduit for this information to be passed out to Division, and for receiving intelligence in return on behalf of C11. But there is a deep distrust amongst many Divisional officers of their colleagues in the impressive, centrally-located tower block which is the Metropolitan Police HQ at New Scotland Yard.

The idea of the FIB is that it serves Divisions first, last and always. Chapman was to run it for two years.

But within months of his taking up the appointment, the pressure of violent crime in London led to the formation of the first AMIP in Area 4.

> There was in 1985 an unprecedented level of murder and other serious crime, particularly in South London, which stretched resources to the limit. I was brought over as an SIO in November, but until 1987 I had also to run the FIB as well as investigating homicide.

One of the first reports to pass across his desk in Croydon police station that autumn was the puzzling disappearance of a highly-regarded London diplomat working for the GLC. However he looked at it, Bob Chapman could not suppress an uneasy suspicion that David Napier Hamilton had disappeared for ever.

David Hamilton was born on 6 August 1930 in the then small Surrey village of Farnham. His family was of the middle- to upper-class caste which for nearly 200 years had produced mandarins to run the Empire and ministers to preach in church. The two Hamilton brothers continued the tradition: Peter, the elder, would become an Anglican vicar in a small Sussex parish, David would see the world as a diplomat.

Early life for David Hamilton followed a very English

pattern. School years at Eton were followed by National Service in the Royal Navy Volunteer Reserve, prior to his going up to Trinity College, Oxford.

In addition to studying for a BA (Honours) degree, David Hamilton found time to pursue an active social life: he was elected, variously, Rear-Commodore of the University Yacht Club, President of the Motor Drivers' Club, the Wine and Food Society, the Trinity Claret Club, and ultimately became Secretary of the Junior Common Room.

He graduated in 1953, and almost immediately left for Africa, to take up the post of mathematics teacher at the General Windgate Secondary School in Addis Ababa, Ethiopia. It was a decisive move: in Ethiopia David Hamilton discovered the two overriding passions that would come to dominate his life – Africa itself, and the young black boys who survived its immutable poverty. It was his taste for the latter which would one day cost him his life.

But although Hamilton was both an enthusiastic homosexual and an energetic paedophile he managed to conceal both from his employers and colleagues throughout his life: certainly those early years in Africa passed uneventfully. In 1955 he transferred from the schoolroom to the lecture theatre, taking up a new post at the Imperial Naval College in Massawa. It marked the start of his seemingly effortless rise through the ranks of post-colonial public service.

The emerging career civil servant spent only a year at the Naval College before crossing the continent for a new post – Executive Officer at the Capricorn Society, an organisation founded to promote multi-racial development throughout Africa, in Salisbury, Rhodesia. The contacts he made in these latter years of the decade served him in good stead: as the 1960s dawned David Hamilton was appointed Private Secretary to Patrick Buchan Hepburn, Governor-General of the West Indies. For two years the mysteries and tensions of Africa were to be supplanted by the comforts offered by Trinidad and Tobago.

Amongst those comforts was a small-time thief and juvenile

delinquent called Kingsley Ignatius Rotardier. By the age of 12 – when Hamilton took him as a bed partner – Rotardier had already earnt himself a criminal record for stealing a bottle of rum from a local store. His father, a respectable if far from wealthy tailor, stood the $25 bond subsequently imposed by the court.

Hamilton's sexual abuse of Rotardier – for that is what their relationship amounted to – continued throughout his two-year posting in Port of Spain. But in 1963 he left the West Indies to return to Africa. He must have assumed he would never see the young boy again. For the next two years the diplomat lectured throughout East and Central Africa, and if he indulged his taste for youthful black company no one apparently noticed or objected.

Between 1965 and 1968 David Hamilton settled back in Ethiopia, first as Commanding Officer of the Imperial Naval College, then as special advisor to the Navy on training and management. Only then did he return to England, fifteen years after adopting Africa as his home.

When he arrived back in London in 1968 he brought with him an impressive pedigree of public service, a certain expertise in African diplomacy, and a sizeable collection of child pornography made or bought during his exile from England. If the years between leaving Oxford and coming back to London had seen Hamilton commit himself to definite liberal politics, they had done nothing to dim his passion for young black adolescents.

Almost immediately he took up the reins of his former academic career. He was first appointed lecturer in liberal studies at South East London Technical College, and then – in 1971 – visiting lecturer in liberal studies at Westminster Technical College.

Three years later he added a PhD to his list of qualifications. His thesis was titled 'Ethiopia's Frontiers, the Boundary Agreements, and their Demarcation, 1896 to 1956'. It reflected his unique combination of academic gifts and diplomatic skills, and drew him to the notice of the Greater London Council which was then about to advertise a new job.

If ever anyone was born to become Head of Protocol and Ceremonies Officer for the Chairman of the GLC, it was David Napier Hamilton. Pictures reveal him to have had that slightly angular gait which is the hallmark of the true English diplomat. His handwriting was painstaking and exquisitely Italianate. Above all he had met, befriended and occasionally worked for any number of African dignitaries. At the beginning of an era which marked the Council's increasing international consciousness – and an enthusiastic embracing of the Third World – Hamilton was the perfect choice.

He took up his office with the quiet enthusiasm that marked his attitude to life – a benign 'Sir Humphrey' running his department efficiently and calmly. His contacts, too, were distinguished; many became personal friends. He was on first-name terms with, amongst others, Princess Margaret, Arch-bishop Trevor Huddleston and the Emperor Haile Selassie.

Much was later to be made of his royal associations. But the reality was faintly mundane. One of his occasional duties at County Hall was to liaise between the Palace and the GLC, and it was in this context that he met Princess Margaret. Evidently he impressed her, for she recommended him to Prince Charles as a suitable future candidate as the Prince's private secretary. Nothing ever came of the suggestion, and David Hamilton continued happily with his work for the Council.

As he left the reception for the Gambian minister that Sunday night in November 1985, Hamilton reminded his employers that he would not be in the office the next week. 'He was taking a short holiday,' recalls Illtyd Harrington, the deputy leader. 'He seemed his normal self – charming and witty.'

But although David Hamilton was taking time off from council business, he was not planning on relaxing completely. His diary for the following day – Monday, 18 November – shows a typically busy schedule of personal and political appointments.

10.00 am: Dentist
Lunch: Peter Hurford [a friend]
2.30 pm: Peace Pagoda Meeting with Trevor Huddleston
6.00 pm: Anglo-Ethiopian Society meeting
8.00 pm: SDP meeting

David Hamilton finally got home at 11.00 pm that night. He
lived in – and owned the freehold of – a large house at 164,
Brixton Road. The building was divided into three separate
homes: Hamilton occupied the basement and ground floor,
letting out the first and second floors to tenants. He also owned
a garage, set back just behind the house. He rented this to a car
mechanic, Austin Douglas.

As David Hamilton arrived home, Douglas was locking up
the garage. The two men were on friendly terms and chatted
for a few moments. Those words were the last ever recorded
from David Napier Hamilton.

Although an energetic and extremely active homosexual,
Hamilton rarely allowed his lovers to stay with him: he was
determined that his sexuality should not become public knowledge.

But since September the fastidious mandarin had had a
lodger. His guest was a friend from his past. Kingsley Ignatius
Rotardier had come to stay.

The years since 1963 when Hamilton had left his youthful
lover in Port of Spain had been less than successful for
Kingsley Rotardier. He had emigrated at some point – his
record is silent on the precise date – to America, settling finally
in New York.

He survived the only way he knew how: a brittle mixture of
charm, deception, threats and theft. He was not, it seems, very
successful: he chalked up his first US conviction in 1968. On 12
November that year he was given a conditional discharge for
one count of criminal possession of stolen property and one of
violent harassment.

According to his own Curriculum Vitae he was simultaneously retained – under a pseudonym – as the official
designer for a theatrical management agency, and worked

extensively with such major music stars as Neil Diamond and Frankie Valley and the Four Seasons.

In his spare time he apparently wrote plays, song lyrics and melodies, became artistic director of New York's Theatre Workshop and was retained as 'director–choreographer' of an off-Broadway musical show. The CV – evidently written in the autumn of 1986 – makes impressive reading:

> Mr Rotardier has songs published by Godspell Music Company, Music Maximus Ltd and The Entertainment Company of New York. His songs have been performed by the world renowned Norman Le Boff Chorale and the Boston Pops. He is an elected member of New York's Dramatists' Guild and the Author's League of America . . .

The document was almost entirely a fantasy.

In part this reflected his flamboyant – and at times unstable– personality: for the rest it was simply part of his existence on the edges of New York's relentless criminal world. Lying became second nature, dishonesty a way of life.

On 19 December 1974 he was sentenced to sixty days' jail for two counts of the American theft offence of Grand Larceny; eighteen months later a three-year sentence followed, this time for inter-state transportation of stolen securities.

Upon his release Rotardier married. But the relationship did not last and he again became a drifter, surviving on his wits and a considerable ability to talk his way into people's lives – and then out of them again when trouble struck.

Ostensibly he made his living in the early 1980s as a fashion model for international houses such as Ralph Lauren and Bill Blass. As a sideline – or so he claims – he variously acted in TV commercials or worked as a make-up artist on broadcast programmes. Chapman's team found it impossible to confirm or refute these boasts.

When, that September in 1985, he arrived in London at David Hamilton's house in Brixton Road, he was supposed to be seeking backing for a Pop Opera which he claimed to have written. Whether or not it ever existed, Kingsley Rotardier gradually began taking over Hamilton's life. The once discreet 55-year-old mandarin was soon to be observed dancing the nights away in the Stallions Club in the established gay clubland of Charing Cross.

His friends became increasingly concerned by this complete change in behaviour. Concern became overt worry at dinner parties which the two men hosted in Brixton Road. David Hamilton, the once confident civil servant, seemed distinctly nervous and ill-at-ease in the company of his young 'friend'.

Kingsley Rotardier, by his own account, knew the reason: Hamilton had apparently confided in him that he feared he had AIDS. Among the appointments he had made for Monday 18 November – though curiously this was not recorded in his diary – was with a clinic to undergo tests. Or so, at least, Rotardier was to suggest.

Rotardier arrived home at 1.20 the following morning. He apparently found Hamilton sitting disconsolate and sobbing in the basement bedroom: the tests had proved positive, and he was carrying the HIV infection which would ultimately lead to a slow and painful death. He told his lover that he had decided to leave Britain early the next morning to visit a special clinic owned by another friend in Hanover, Dr Runkle. Rotardier claimed that he left the house within three hours and caught the 6.00 am flight to Germany.

The process of explaining David Hamilton's abrupt departure began later the same day. At 10.00 am Austin Douglas arrived at the house, following his usual working routine. As he walked up the path he was stopped by Rotardier who recounted the events in the basement bedroom.

At 10.30 am Rotardier telephoned Hamilton's secretary, Margaret Beckett, and mumbled a brief and incoherent message to the effect that her boss was gravely ill with a blood problem and had gone to Paris for tests. The information puzzled Beckett: Hamilton had telephoned her the previous day about a letter he had dictated. He had seemed in good spirits, and had mentioned that he would call in on the Tuesday morning to sign the note.

Thirty minutes later Rotardier asked Douglas to drive him to the GLC to take some documents to Hamilton's employers. The documents turned out to be a letter of resignation.

At some point in the early afternoon Rotardier returned to the house and bumped into Stephen Wright, one of the tenants. Wright noticed that the normally bumptious model seemed shocked and shaken, and when Rotardier explained Hamilton's abrupt departure, suggested that he come upstairs for supper that night.

Rotardier appeared grateful, and agreed to join Wright and his wife Pari after 9.30 pm. He also explained that he would be going away – to see Hamilton in Hanover – the next morning, taking a British Airways flight from Gatwick.

By the time Kingsley Rotardier walked up to the Wrights' flat, however, he seemed to have regained his composure. So much so that when, close to midnight, they were joined by a mutual friend, Rotardier agreed to go dancing with him on the spot.

The friend was a black actor called Carl Andrews. He had briefly enjoyed a profitable career playing a car mechanic in the ITV soap opera, *Crossroads*. He had also been the cause of some friction between Hamilton and Rotardier. The friction had developed through jealousy: Hamilton became increasingly unhappy at the growing friendship between his two closest black friends: Andrews and Rotardier became almost inseparable.

As it turned out, Rotardier's proposed flight to Hamilton's bedside was postponed for several days – days which he filled by going out shopping and dutifully cleaning the house. He finally bought his ticket in an Oxford Street travel agency on Friday, 22 November. It was valid for travel the next day, and early that Saturday morning he made his way to the airport.

The house at 164, Brixton Road was not left empty, however: Rotardier had invited his sister Valewska and her daughter to stay. It was a move that surprised the Wrights and Austin Douglas, who bumped into the women later that afternoon.

But what surprised him more was the smell inside the house.

David Hamilton had been proud of – if not meticulous about – his home, yet when the mechanic called there he reeled back from an overpowering and most unpleasant smell. It reminded him of rotting meat.

Later that evening he went to supper with the Wrights' and told them about the smell. The three friends decided they would wait until Valewska left the house and then go in to explore.

At a little after 11.00 pm they heard the front door close and slipped downstairs with a spare key. Almost immediately they were hit by the pungent smell. They held their handkerchiefs tight against their faces and walked on towards its apparent source. The smell was at its strongest outside the kitchen door. Beyond was a staircase which led down to the basement; they tried the handle, but it was securely locked. All three were by now convinced that there was a body lying somewhere in the house. The most likely location seemed to be in the basement, the most likely candidate David Napier Hamilton.

What made their amateur detective instincts sharper was the unusual degree of tidiness throughout the house – except for the bathroom which was uncharacteristically filthy. The lounge carpet seemed to have been shampooed and then given an extra chemical application of some description: the pile smelt of 'Shake and Vac'.

The Wrights and Douglas agreed to return the next morning once they had found a key to the basement. When they did, they searched it thoroughly, but in vain. There was nothing out of the ordinary, except for the persistent and still overpowering smell. As far as the reluctant sleuths could tell this emanated from behind the central heating boiler.

Whatever their suspicions, without a body there was little else for the three friends to do except wait – either for David Hamilton to get in touch, or for Kingsley Rotardier to return.

Rotardier was the first to make contact. On Monday, 25 November he telephoned Austin Douglas to say he was in Hanover and had seen Hamilton. The gist of the call was that although Hamilton was ill, he was anxious that his friends should not worry themselves. Rotardier appeared more concerned with the problems he was apparently having in arranging a return flight from Hanover.

For the next two days, Rotardier phoned Douglas with the same story. Always he had seen Hamilton; always he was having trouble getting a flight home. There was one other consistent factor in these phone calls – a high-pitched whine on the line. It did not sound like a European line at all: if Douglas had had to guess Rotardier's location, he would have said it sounded as if the model was calling from America.

Finally, the following Thursday, Rotardier flew into Gatwick at 10.15 am. He made his way back to the house and quickly phoned Margaret Beckett to make an appointment with Hamilton's deputy, Keith Bennett. The secretary fixed the meeting for later the same day, and at 1.00 pm Rotardier announced formally that Hamilton was dying of AIDS and wanted to be left alone.

Bennett was far from happy, and privately gave instructions that the letter of resignation Rotardier had delivered a few days earlier on behalf of his superior was not to be acted on. All the same, he agreed to send on redundancy forms to the house in Brixton.

Meanwhile, Stephen and Pari Wright were becoming more than ever convinced that David Hamilton was dead, and that the smell in the kitchen represented what was left of his mortal remains. They decided to have it out with Rotardier at the first opportunity.

Their chance came the next day. Rotardier called round to say that since he would not be returning to England for some time, Hamilton had asked his lover to collect the rent. Wright refused point blank: he wanted, he said, some written evidence that Rotardier had authority to act on his landlord's behalf. Failing that he and his wife would only pay the rent directly into Hamilton's private bank account. A heated argument was the only outcome.

Or at least that was as far as Rotardier was aware. At some

point in those early days after David Hamilton disappeared, someone began talking to the police.

Bob Chapman, then both an SIO at the newly-created 4 AMIP and in charge of the Force Intelligence Bureau, will now say only that he 'became aware' of suspicions about the missing mandarin late in November 1985.

> People were concerned that Hamilton wasn't around any
> more, and that Rotardier seemed to be taking over the
> running of his life in his absence. But we had no formal report
> of a missing person – much less a dead body – and we were
> simultaneously coping with a large increase in murders and
> other violent crime.
>   I decided to keep an eye on the situation, and on Rotardier.
> He seemed to be travelling about a lot, so the obvious course
> of action was to look at his credit card records, to see what
> cards he was using to go where.

Kingsley Rotardier was, in fact, about to set off on his travels once again. On Wednesday, 4 December he bought an air ticket to Hanover and flew out the next day.

What made Chapman particularly interested in the transaction – and more than a dozen like it since the disappearance nearly three weeks before – was that the name on the credit card used to pay the bills was not Kingsley Rotardier: it was David Napier Hamilton. Either the diplomat was not in Hanover – in which case why should Rotardier announce that he was? – or Rotardier was making free with his lover's credit cards. The detective decided to keep a very close watch on the mysterious credit card slips.

Within days of Rotardier arriving in Germany letters began to filter back to England, apparently from David Hamilton. Each tried to reassure the recipients that they should not worry on his account. Austin Douglas's letter raised more suspicions than it allayed: the note was handwritten, mentioning that its author planned to relocate from Hanover to Paris within the coming weeks. But the writing seemed quite unlike David Hamilton's copybook script.

Rotardier flew home within twenty-four hours, as up to half

a dozen other letters were making their way through the European postal system. For the next week he lived in the house in Brixton Road as if he owned it.

Indeed an open letter dated 4 December, and seemingly signed by Hamilton in Germany, gave him wide-ranging financial authority. In particular it provided for Rotardier to use his lover's credit cards.

And use them he did. Chapman began accumulating a stack of slips from Barclaycard, Access and Diners' Club. A similar pattern emerged from cashpoint machines: Kingsley Rotardier was making free with the dwindling funds in David Hamilton's bank account, in addition to buying meals in expensive restaurants on the credit cards. Curiously, his often clumsy forgeries of Hamilton's signature went undetected.

There were two transactions in particular which strengthened the detective's suspicions. The first had taken place on 19 November itself – the day Hamilton had apparently flown out of London in search of treatment in Hanover. Rotardier had said that his lover's flight had been at 6.00 am: yet a credit card receipt seemed to show that later in the day he had bought a meat cleaver and saw from a kitchen equipment supplier in South London.

The second was stranger still. Another receipt showed that someone – Chapman presumed it was Rotardier – had used Hamilton's card to buy an airline ticket on 23 November. In itself – and if Chapman's assumption was correct – that was evidence of Rotardier fraudulently making free with his friend's money before he had written authority. But it was the destination of the air flight which jarred: Rotardier had said he was flying to Hamilton's bedside in Hanover. Why then was the ticket for a journey to New York?

On Thursday, 12 December Stephen Wright finally managed to confront Rotardier with his suspicions. He had gone downstairs in the hope of 'clearing the air' as he later told Chapman. Rotardier reacted strongly and began to argue violently. Wright was supported by his wife, and by Florence Wakelin, Hamilton's elderly cleaning lady. Where, they wanted to know, was the evidence that Hamilton had gone to Hanover?

Rotardier pulled out a British Airways flight voucher and began to wave it in their faces. This, he asserted, proved what he had been telling them. Stephen Wright was not convinced and asked to examine the ticket: Rotardier adamantly refused.

The row was only defused by another old friend of David Hamilton called Paul de Swardt, a computer operator for IBM who had spent much of the past year living in Amsterdam, and was currently on holiday in London. He assured the Wrights that Hamilton was alive, implied that they had spoken recently on the telephone and that he had personally made the trip from Holland to tell them so. In fact, no such telephone call had been made by David Hamilton. The telephone conversation had been with Kingsley Rotardier, who explained that he was having trouble with the Wrights and – on David's behalf – wanted de Swardt to stall them for a while. The key to this apparently implausible proposition was a mysterious list which the model claimed the mandarin had given him in Germany. On it were the names of those whom Hamilton apparently wanted to be kept informed as to his progress, and – by contrast – those whom he wanted to be given very little information indeed. Paul de Swardt, for the time at least, belonged in the first category; the Wrights were firmly located in the second.

Kingsley Rotardier occupied himself for the next week by undertaking a gruelling round of shopping trips in the West End, and arranging flight tickets and visas for a forthcoming trip. He was planning to spend the week before Christmas in New York: but first he had a brief visit to make to Paris – ostensibly to see David Hamilton once again.

His French sojourn lasted precisely fifteen hours. By 9.45 pm on Wednesday, 18 December he was back at Heathrow. Less than twenty-four hours later he flew out to New York.

Throughout December Chapman had been assembling an every-growing mountain of credit card slips, all bearing the name of David Hamilton, but all quite clearly signed by someone else. Kingsley Rotardier's efforts at forging his lover's signature varied from the passable to the very poor indeed. Chapman decided to ask for cooperation from the card companies' American offices: he wanted to know what the model would find to buy in New York, and how often he would use the cards.

> Unfortunately they were not at all helpful. They said there was an issue of confidentiality – something to do with the Freedom of Information Act, it seems – that prevented them from giving the details. Inevitably that just delayed actions I wanted to take.

That action amounted to a holding charge of fraud. Chapman was by now convinced that Rotardier had murdered his lover and somehow disposed of the body. But without a formal missing persons report – and no one had yet made one – or without the body itself, he would not be able to arrest the model on suspicion of murder. The fraudulent use of Hamilton's credit cards was the ideal opportunity to open the case up. But as yet there was not enough to go on. For the next few months Chapman had to sit still and watch as the drama unfolded.

Kingsley Rotardier arrived back in Britain on Boxing Day, together with a teenager he called his son. In fact, though the boy did not know it, Rotardier was not his real father. Nonetheless, the pair settled in to a comfortable routine at 164, Brixton Road. As ever, Rotardier lived off Hamilton's credit cards and bank account, and at the same time began attending functions on his behalf, including a party held by the Anglo-Ethiopian Society.

But as the year drew to a close some pieces of this strange jigsaw were resolutely refusing to fit together. The first to notice was Paul de Swardt.

De Swardt was due to spend the New Year in Paris and had asked Rotardier for Hamilton's address in the city. Somewhat reluctantly the model had told him that Hamilton was living with an Ethiopian friend at 5, Avenue des Chasseurs. De Swardt offered to take out the pile of post which had accumulated for his old friend, but Rotardier brusquely declined the suggestion, claiming already to have sent the mail on.

When he arrived in Paris, De Swardt made his way to the Avenue. He could find absolutely no trace of an English civil servant living anywhere near the given address, but he did discover a name he thought sounded Ethiopian. He rang the bell; there was no reply. Puzzled, he left a card addressed to David Hamilton on the notice board beside the door, listing two telephone numbers where his old friend could get in touch. A few days later, having waited in vain for a phone call, de Swardt went back to Avenue des Chasseurs. The card was still in the same place: it had clearly been neither moved nor read.

The second set of oddities began to arrive via the post throughout late December and the New Year. David Hamilton had apparently decided to end his mysterious silence and write to his friends and colleagues at work.

Or at least he had decided to type letters: virtually all of the correspondence – even belated Christmas cards - was typewritten, bearing only a small and distinctly untypical signature on the bottom.

The reason for this highly unusual style was apparently connected with his illness. In a letter to Tony Banks, then GLC Chairman and now a Labour MP, 'Hamilton' spelled out the problem.

Dear Tony,
My profound gratitude for your very sweet letter of support from you, but as the doctors have advised, I am indeed prepared for the worst.

My biggest worry presently is my appearance, I have lost quite a few pounds, and much more hair since I left London. I can not bear to see my reflection in a mirror, much more face any of my friends and colleagues.

This malady consumes one's body from its inner most areas. I am fighting, it is painful. Especially because my emotional state is still fragile.

Writing takes too much out of me, I was always so eager to write notes and letters before this, but now it takes all the energy and willpower I can produce to write answers to the

> many Christmas cards and letters of concern from so many
> super friends in London . . .

If writing was a trial for the sick man, he managed at least to convey in this letter – and in dozens of others like it – how valuable had been the friendship and support of one man in particular: Kingsley Ignatius Rotardier.

It was to Rotardier, apparently, that the dying Hamilton felt he owed 'his very life'. In his letter to Banks, the patient who was too weak to see his friends managed to ask the GLC Chairman to help Rotardier with a minor passport problem. It bespoke a touching concern for the minutiae of a particular friend's administrative problems.

But there was something not quite right about these letters. For one thing the grammar, phrasing and punctuation bore no resemblance to the punctilious style favoured by the missing civil servant. Sometimes, most curiously, Americanisms crept in: the very English diplomat seemed now to refer to 'checks' rather than 'cheques'. It was all most irregular.

And then there was his apparently deteriorating memory for names and titles. Florrie Wakelin had become far more than a cleaning lady in the years she worked for David Hamilton. In fact by November 1985 although she still turned up regularly to clean the house, the visits had become social occasions: she would take tea and chat with her old friend, before leaving without so much as flicking a duster. It was a touching and gentle ritual both parties enjoyed greatly.

Which made the letter which Florrie received from Paris all the stranger. True, it was emotional and sufficiently intimate to pass muster on content, but the envelope contained a curious mistake. David Hamilton had apparently forgotten how to spell her surname: Wakelin had unaccountably become Wakeland.

There was a similar error on the envelope bearing a long letter to Peter Hamilton. It was perhaps the strangest yet: the former Head of Protocol had apparently decided to address his brother – a Church of England minister – as 'Vicar Peter

Hamilton' rather than the more correct 'Reverend'. It seemed an unlikely mistake.

More than thirty letters and cards found their way back to England from France, all repeating the same message: David Hamilton wanted to be left alone to cope with his illness in his own way. Most suggested that the recipient should trust in Kingsley Rotardier if they wanted to pass on greetings, information or other correspondence.

If all of this seems a paper-thin pretence, then it is perhaps worth remembering that we are viewing the correspondence both with hindsight and in its totality. Each recipient of what purported to be a letter from their old friend had no means of knowing that the errors and strangely jarring language were repeated in dozens of others.

Neither did they know that Rotardier had flown to Paris himself – a fact which might have gone some way to explain so many letters finding their way to London from France. They saw only the sad evidence of a friend losing his faculties and dying of AIDS.

It was an impression reinforced by a letter from a French doctor that Rotardier was able to produce in January 1986. It was intended, apparently, as a type of formal doctor's note for Hamilton's employers at the GLC, who were being asked at the same time by Rotardier for his lover's statutory sick pay. The letter was short and to the point:

> Mr David Napier Hamilton is my patient now for three months. He is very sick and it is impossible for him to work.
> He is receiving treatment in Paris, and it will be necessary for him to be away from his employment for an indefinite time.

The letter was signed 'Guiy Galteau, Medecin', and listed an address at 19, Avenue McMahon. It seemed to support what Rotardier had been saying.

Throughout the January and February of 1986 letters continued to arrive from Paris, while Rotardier continued to live on Hamilton's money in London. Then late in February, a change of scenery was mooted: the dying diplomat had apparently met an extremely pleasant Malaysian at the mysterious clinic he attended, and had agreed to leave France for a religious retreat in a remote Malay village. A letter to Keith Bennett at the GLC explained this, and paved the way for more contact with Kingsley Rotardier.

> My dear Keith,
> Forgive me for not getting back to you sooner, but with plans to journey to Malaysia as well as clinic every other day and the required rest period, honestly I have put things off. To start with I have been inundated with mail since everyone seems to have gotten hold of my address. I have asked Kingsley to pick up my effects and personal papers . . .

It was the shock of so many of his friends discovering his location – a shock which again seems to have resulted in curiously American phrasing – that had led him to seek the peace of an unidentified Malay village. Hamilton's friends began asking Kingsley Rotardier what he knew of this mysterious new Malaysian friend who had adopted the sick man: all Rotardier could tell them was that there was a forwarding address – c/o Marchal Yunus, Mats Yunus, or Mohd Dahan in Badak Kuala, Terengganu.

Eventually this was expanded to the full address and a telephone number. Peter Hamilton rang it: he had some difficulty in explaining to the voice at the other end what he wanted and decided to write a letter. It was returned unopened some weeks later.

It would be Peter Hamilton who finally started the formal investigation by 4 AMIP: on 3 March 1986, David Hamilton was formally reported missing.

It turned out to be just the invitation Bob Chapman needed. After local police had carried out a few cursory and routine enquiries he began to assemble a team within the AMIP which would investigate the presumed murder of the missing mandarin. First in the detective's sights was Kingsley Rotardier.

The interviews between the male model and the experienced
investigator read like classical set-pieces of the interrogator's
art: Rotardier, arrogant, aggressive and obstructive;
Chapman, calm, quiet and rigorous.

By April the detective had enough formally to enter charges
of fraudulent use of Hamilton's credit cards. Rotardier was
cautioned, advised of his rights and bailed to appear at court
the following December. The credit cards were also confiscated,
effectively cutting off his supply of funds. If the slim, arrogant
model was behind the suspicious correspondence from various
parts of the globe, Chapman reasoned, he would no longer be
able to travel to set up the arrangements. From April onward
he would have to rely on whatever mechanisms he had
managed to create to date.

In fact the letters continued to arrive, now postmarked
Malaysia. They appeared to bear out Rotardier's version of
Hamilton's decision to seek solace in a remote village. Together
with the continually increasing burden of work at the AMIP's
Croydon HQ – this, after all, was the period when Michele Lupo
had embarked upon serial murder – it was enough to delay a
full-scale murder investigation.

There was also the continuing lack of a body. Chapman knew
that it was extremely rare, not to mention decidedly difficult, to
obtain a murder conviction while the victim's corpse remained
undiscovered.

It's not unknown in legal history for the police to get a
conviction for murder without finding the body, but it
obviously makes the job much more difficult.

There were three recent cases which gave me a precedent.
In 1969 two men were convicted of the murder of Muriel
McKay, though no corpse was ever found. In 1984 Louise
Brown, a Downs syndrome baby, was allegedly snatched from
a car and disappeared: eventually several of her family were
convicted of manslaughter. And the following year Ronald
Barton was successfully prosecuted for the murder of his
step-daughter without any evidence of death being
presented.

So it was possible; if we were to go through with the

investigation we would simply need overwhelming
circumstantial evidence to be sure of convicting the right
killer.

Although officially 4 AMIP did not begin a formal
murder investigation until January 1987, it is clear that Bob
Chapman had just such a prospect firmly in mind from as early
as February 1986. Quietly and carefully he began examining
and unpicking the strands of the enormously complicated web
Kingsley Rotardier had woven around the disappearance of his
lover.

The first points to establish centred around the last known
twenty-four hours of David Hamilton's life. Chapman began
enquiring about the mysterious AIDS test – an examination
not recorded in Hamilton's diary.

> Hamilton was meant to have had the test on the Monday and
> obtained the information that he was infected with the
> disease later same day. When we checked we quickly
> established that it would have been impossible – quite
> impossible – for the results to have been obtained that
> quickly.
> So we were left with another mystery: either the story was
> untrue, or he had undergone the tests some time before. We
> then checked with all his known medical advisors. None of
> them reported seeing him for any reason connected with
> AIDS. The most we got back was that Hamilton had
> consulted one about a touch of lumbago.

Next there was the strange purchase of the meat cleaver and
saw on 19 November. Chapman discovered that they had been
paid for with Hamilton's Barclaycard. Since he could now
prove that only one person had been abusing the missing man's
credit cards, the evidence seemed to suggest that Kingsley
Rotardier had made the purchase.

The same thought had occurred to Paul de Swardt's wife,
Mary. She had discovered the implements in the kitchen at
164 Brixton Road just before Christmas 1985, and – since they
seemed more than a little out of place – had asked Rotardier
about them. He explained that just before David Hamilton

disappeared the couple had decided to clear out the freezer together. Among the tasty morsels was a packet of frozen cow-heels – a discovery which prompted Rotardier to make a Caribbean meal. Because the regular stock of knives and utensils in Hamilton's kitchen were not sufficiently strong, he decided to buy a cleaver.

On the surface it sounded a reasonable story: but Mary de Swardt knew David Hamilton's kitchen well. She knew, for example, that he kept a special frozen meat blade attachment for his electric carving knife: it would have been more than strong enough for the task. Additionally, Rotardier seemed to have forgotten about the saw: no mention was made of, nor explanation offered for, its purchase.

As a final check, Chapman sought out airline records for Tuesday, 19 November – the morning on which David Hamilton allegedly caught an early flight to Hanover. There was no mention of his name anywhere on any operator's rosters.

Similarly, the flight to Hanover which Rotardier claimed to have made four days later turned out to have taken him to New York. Why had he phoned Austin Douglas every day for three days, pretending to be in Germany?

By the time Rotardier came to court in January 1987, facing the fraud charges stemming from his abuse of Hamilton's credit cards, Chapman had enough to go on to charge him with murder.

All the evidence suggested David Hamilton had not – could not have – left Britain in the way, and for the reasons, Rotardier suggested. An advert placed by Peter Hamilton the previous November had yielded not a single reply. The day Rotardier pleaded guilty to deception and received a nine-month suspended jail sentence, the murder enquiry was ready to begin.

Chapman set up a dedicated major investigation incident room at Brixton police station. From the local division he borrowed a detective inspector. The remainder of the team comprised two sergeants and two detective constables, plus an office staff of five. It was a pitifully small squad to investigate a case that stretched across Europe to America and the Far East.

The first task was to assemble all the evidence of alleged contacts from Hamilton since his disappearance. Piece by piece the team began putting together a complicated jigsaw of letters and cards from a variety of addresses in Germany, France and Malaysia. Added to these were conversations which Hamilton's friends reported with Rotardier in which he claimed either to have seen or had telephone contact with the missing diplomat.

The AMIP began listing these on a chronological spread-sheet, showing exactly where Hamilton was alleged to have been in any given week. Next, they began researching Rotardier's movements: when these were entered on the spreadsheet an interesting pattern developed. In the first three months after the disappearance, wherever Hamilton appeared to be based, Rotardier visited. In itself that might not have been surprising – the men after all were lovers, and Hamilton's letters, if genuine, suggested Rotardier had become his sole supporting friend.

But it was the timing which was revealing. Hamilton's letters giving a forwarding address began arriving only *after* Rotardier had flown in – and then out again. Chapman began to suspect that Rotardier had set up a series of forwarding arrangements for letters that he himself had written and dropped off on his flying visits. The theory held good for both Germany and France: only Malaysia proved a puzzle – the AMIP team could find no evidence that Rotardier had ever visited the country.

The Malaysian angle took a new twist when Chapman interviewed Peter Hamilton. The vicar told the detective that in the summer of 1986 he had received a telephone call from Valewska, Rotardier's sister. She had said David Hamilton had sent word from Malaysia that he would be returning to London by the end of June.

But by August David Hamilton had not appeared. If he was back in London he had failed to make contact with any of his close friends or relatives. Except, that is, Kingsley Rotardier.

On 8 August, as he arrived for a routine committal hearing on the fraud charges, Rotardier was able to tell the vicar that he had seen his brother at a birthday lunch in London a few days previously. Hamilton had, it appeared, returned to Britain on 20 June and moved in with a male nurse living in a Fairfax Road in North London – but Rotardier claimed that he had no more precise details.

Chapman decided to split his enquiries into five geographical areas – London, Paris, Germany, America and Malaysia. It was a brave decision given the limited resources available to him and an inevitably inadequate budget. As an additional check he decided to commission both fingerprint tests and handwriting analysis on the alleged David Hamilton letters which had been sent from around the world.

The first enquiries to yield positive results were the investigations into Rotardier's antecedents. John Scullion, the detective inspector whom Chapman had borrowed from Brixton, quickly established that in addition to his known criminal convictions, Kingsley Rotardier had been involved in another brush with the law. The charge had been murder.

On Valentine's Day, 1975, Francine McDougal was found dead in her own home in New York. Whoever killed her had been thorough: Mrs McDougal had been bludgeoned with a blunt instrument, stabbed with a knife, strangled with a ligature and finally drowned in the bath. The autopsy report listed cause of death as asphyxia by drowning, depressed fractures of the skull and ligature strangulation.

The motive for the murder had been robbery, and there had been a witness. Shortly after the killing Detective Francis Donnelly of Manhattan South Task Force took a statement from Mrs McDougal's 16-year-old son Victor. It was revealing:

> I left home about 1230 hours on 14 February 1975, and got home about 1300 hours. The door to the kitchen was open, I entered and saw my [elder] brother Juan just standing, not saying anything. I saw Kingsley standing over my mother who was on the floor in the hallway in a pool of blood.
> I said, 'What are you doing?' Kingsley punched me and told

me he would kill me and my whole family if I ever talked. I
went to my mother's bedroom, picked up scissors to protect
myself and called the police. I heard Kingsley drag my
mother down the hall to the bathroom. When I got off the
phone they [Kingsley and Juan] had run out of the house.

Juan was, in fact, Victor's half-brother and most usually
used the surname Alcantara. Kingsley was, of course
Rotardier. A search of the home they shared yielded a
collection of bloodstained clothing.

The case would have been watertight had it not been for two
serious problems. First, the Manhattan detectives had not
obtained a fully-authorised search warrant to turn over
Rotardier's apartment – the evidence of the blood-stained
clothing was rejected as legally inadmissible into court.

Additionally, Victor was far from the perfect witness. He was
mentally slow, and clearly terrified of Rotardier. A decision was
reached that the only way he would testify would be under
hypnosis. He did so and duly identified Rotardier and
Alcantara. But the jury decided that the hypnosis made his
evidence unreliable. Both Juan Alcantara and Kingsley
Rotardier walked free from the court-house.

On its own – though, doubtless interesting – the information
was far from conclusive in the AMIP enquiry. But the name
Alcantara began to figure prominently in Bob Chapman's
European investigation.

In Germany he had quickly established both Rotardier's
movements in Hanover and the fact that there was no doctor
with a name remotely like the one which Rotardier claimed
Hamilton had gone to stay with. Next stop was France and the
second 'doctor', Guiy Galteau.

According to the Council of the National Order of Doctors,
there was no record of a Guiy Galteau registered as a
practitioner anywhere in France. When we went to the
address listed on the letterhead – 19, Avenue McMahon, in
Paris – we found it to be occupied by a Monsieur François
Marchal. He had lived there since 1975 and had never heard
of anyone called Galteau.

But the name Marchal rang a bell in Chapman's mind. He looked back through the case files until he found what he wanted: the name on the Malaysian forwarding address for David Hamilton was Marchal Yunus.

The germ of an idea was taking root in the investigation: if Rotardier had, as the detectives believed, faked bogus letters from Hamilton to his friends and organised a complicated system of forwarding agents, then the clues might be in the vicinity of each known address. Chapman checked the records for the rest of Avenue McMahon. He found no Guiy Galteau; but he did discover an Alcantara.

Juan Alcantara, the man acquitted with Rotardier of his mother's murder in 1975, had moved from New York to Paris, married and produced a son. But the relationship began to fall apart as Juan admitted to his wife a homosexual relationship back in Manhattan. His lover then had been Kingsley Rotardier. By the end of 1985 the couple were living apart; Josyanne Alcantara remained in the matrimonial home with their son. Her address was 9, Avenue McMahon.

Chapman set about interviewing her and her estranged husband. He quickly discovered that Rotardier had bought them both a meal when he arrived in Paris in January 1986 – two months after David Hamilton disappeared, and one month before letters bearing his name arrived home in England.

Juan Alcantara furnished three other vital pieces of information. The first was his former telephone number in Paris. He had owned the number until July 1985 when he had separated from his wife. It was exactly this number which the mysterious Dr Guiy Galteau quoted on his headed notepaper.

Then there was the question of that name – Galteau. Chapman asked Alcantara if he had ever heard of it before. The American was not quite sure, but he *thought* it was the maiden name of a friend's mother. The friend turned out to be Kingsley Rotardier.

Alcantara's last helpful comment proved to be the most valuable of all. He told Chapman that he had introduced

Rotardier to another friend in Paris, a man called Robert Tissot. The purpose of the introduction was so that Rotardier could continue to send letters to him without Josyanne finding out. The Alcantaras might be separated, but Juan evidently still harboured faith in the future of their relationship.

Chapman was keen to contact Robert Tissot for one reason above all others. His address was 5, Avenue des Chasseurs – the same address given on all letters from David Hamilton since February 1986.

Tissot, when contacted, told a slightly different story from Alcantara. Yes, he confirmed, Juan had introduced Mr Rotardier to him. But the male model made it clear that he wanted to use the address as a contact point for David Hamilton's friends.

Rotardier told Tissot that Hamilton did not want his family and friends to see him, and so the fiction of a French address was needed. Rotardier would send letters on to Avenue des Chasseurs, and Tissot would, in turn, re-mail them back to 164, Brixton Road. In this way a French franking imprint would appear on each. What he failed to tell the Frenchman was that the letters in question would come not from Hamilton's friends, but from Rotardier, pretending to be the reclusive civil servant. Chapman recalls:

> We were able to find a link for every name and address in Paris – except one. The one that foxed us was 'Guiy' as in Galteau. It was a highly unusual spelling and, having cracked Rotardier's system, it had to have been inspired by someone or something in Paris.

The answer, when it came, proved Chapman right. Rotardier had also been introduced to a Paris-based confidence trickster called Guiy de Montford. The pattern continued, the jigsaw pieces began to fit together.

Next, the AMIP team turned its attention to the Malaysian connection. Chapman decided to send out his 'bagman', Sergeant David Cooper (later to be promoted to inspector and

to work on the Noel Christopher murder) and another AMIP
sergeant, Terence Owen.

The pair had relatively little to go on when, in March 1987,
they arrived in Malaysia. The first priority was to check out the
address David Hamilton had allegedly given as a contact point
in Terengganu.

The address in question turned out to be the office of a
Malaysian businessman called Dahan Bin Yunus. Not only did
the name match the one which Hamilton had passed on via
Rotardier to his friends, but the Malay had indeed met the
missing diplomat.

But at that point the lead petered out. Yunus's encounter
with Hamilton had been in the late 1970s when the diplomat
had visited the East Coast resort of Terengganu on holiday.
Yunus had been sitting on the beach when Hamilton had
approached him and struck up a friendship.

However, that was the last time they had met: he certainly
had not seen the Englishman this year – or for several years
before it. All he could tell Cooper was that a letter had recently
arrived for Hamilton from England and that someone had rung
his office asking for the missing civil servant.

Next, the detectives began checking for religious communities similar to the one Hamilton – again via Rotardier –
said he had joined. There were none. Further, they were
assured both that Malay custom would make it virtually
impossible for a western white man to live undetected in their
villages for any length of time, and that because each
Malaysian citizen was forced to carry identification and show it
to the police on demand, someone would surely have noticed
him. Cooper was baffled.

> It was quite clear – from immigration records as well as all
> the rest of the information – that David Hamilton wasn't in
> Malaysia. We also checked the country's AIDS records – it
> had only five cases and none of those were westerners.
> Certainly no Englishman was registered as having died in
> the relevant period. But still we couldn't answer the question
> of how letters purporting to come from Hamilton had been
> posted in Malaysia.

The answer, when they finally stumbled upon it, was depressingly simple.

John Michael George Haines worked as a reservation assistant for Malaysian Airlines in London. He was also a homosexual and, sometime early in 1986, had gone to Stallions nightclub in Charing Cross Road. There he had met and was befriended by Kingsley Rotardier.

The friendship continued until, in April that year, Rotardier mentioned his friend David Hamilton who was dying of AIDS. He explained how the mandarin from the GLC had suddenly quit Britain to avoid telling his friends and family, but he now needed to move to Malaysia away from prying eyes, to die in peace. Malaysia seemed perfect as a cover story: he really intended to return to London.

> Rotardier asked Haines to arrange for letters to be posted from Malaysia to England. At first Haines was concerned and would not agree, but after some persuasion he gave in, provided he could examine the letters beforehand.
>   When he was satisfied he gave the letters – four in all, addressed to Rotardier, Hamilton's bank and Peter Hamilton – to another airline employee who was due to travel to Malaysia on holiday. All the letters were typewritten; all were handed to him by Kingsley Rotardier.

The jigsaw was almost complete. The international pieces fit together. All that was left was the London end.

While the international enquiries were going on, simple forensic tests had been carried out on a number of the mounting pieces of evidence. The first check had been for fingerprints on the letters received from David Hamilton by his friends and relations. Several had an exact match for one of Rotardier's fingerprints. Yet ostensibly the young male model had never seen, much less handled, the correspondence.

Next, Chapman called in experts in handwriting analysis, first to examine the credit card signatures then the letters themselves. The credit card slips proved easy: signature expert Christopher Davies was able to testify categorically that the real David Hamilton had not signed any of the vouchers which had accumulated since 18 November 1985.

The handwriting analysis was less straightfoward. Chapman called in Janet Whitcut, an established lexicographer with a substantial academic record of linguistic analysis. Her function was not to analyse the actual handwriting – there was precious little of that since most of the letters were typed – but to investigate the content word by word and compare it with Hamilton's known writing style. It was a new departure for Chapman and, so far as the Metropolitan Police could discover, for any British murder investigation.

Mrs Whitcut's evidence showed that there were 'striking differences' in style between documents Hamilton was known to have written prior to his disappearance, and those letters which Rotardier maintained he had penned thereafter.

Typewriter tests proved more conclusive still. In the corner of a room at 164, Brixton Road, the AMIP team found an old typewriter which subsequent examination proved to have created several of the letters sent to Hamilton's family and friends between December 1985 and spring 1986.

Chapman had become convinced that his case against Rotardier was watertight. To be certain he ordered police sniffer dogs into 164, Brixton Road. It was late in the investigation – more than a year had passed since the disappearance, but even so the test proved positive. Police dog Scarlet had been specially trained to detect the smell of human remains: as she searched the ground floor and basement area – where the Wrights and Austin Douglas had smelled what they thought was rotting meat – she stopped twice – once by the fireplace and once near the bath.

> I personally believe that Rotardier killed David Hamilton
> probably by strangling him or perhaps with a knife, and then
> cut up his body with the cleaver and the saw. I think he then
> burnt the body in an incinerator in the garden.

The basis for Chapman's belief in the latter gruesome disposal technique stemmed from a statement made by Stephen and

Pari Wright. Late on the night of Monday 18 November, the last night Hamilton was seen alive, the Wrights smelt and saw smoke rising from the garden incinerator below their bedroom window. They looked out, puzzled: it was well after midnight and they could not see anyone tending the flames. Nor could they understand why anyone would choose to burn garden rubbish – as they assumed it to be – that late at night.

Chapman had enough. On 5 January 1987 he gave orders for the arrest of Kingsley Ignatius Rotardier on suspicion of murder. The date was no happy accident: Chapman knew Rotardier would be at the Inner London Crown Court on that day to face the fraud charges relating to David Hamilton's credit cards. When the male model was released from the dock, AMIP officers approached and arrested him.

It is part of the skill of an experienced detective to be able to interview suspects carefully, meticulously and without undue pressure. In recent years, and in highly publicised cases, the skill has been sometimes allowed to lapse in favour of out-of-hours tampering with the evidence. Not so with the interviews between Superintendent Bob Chapman and Kingsley Rotardier.

All the meetings were tape recorded, and took place in the presence of Rotardier's solicitor. It is an unnerving experience listening to the recordings now, so it must have been doubly difficult for Chapman and his colleagues.

Rotardier's mood swings wildly from one end of the emotional scale to another. At times he berates the detectives for having the temerity to waste his valuable time with such foolish questions; on other occasions he sits tonelessly parroting the same answer to each question – 'No comment'.

Throughout these lengthy interviews Rotardier stuck to his central story, and constantly challenged the detectives to prove him wrong.

'I know where David Hamilton is,' he boasted frequently, but when pressed to give a location, either clamped his mouth firmly shut or taunted his inquisitors angrily.

'No, find out: you people are doing expert work in the

interests of justice,' was his sarcastic response to one question. Later, as Chapman pressed him on the exact circumstances of Hamilton's disappearance, he spat back:

> Are you telling me that in all your marvellous investigations you did not discover that David purchased a ticket to leave London during that period? Is that what you are telling me? Is that what you upstanding gentlemen are telling me? . . .
> Don't ask me anything, don't ask me anything, do you understand me? . . . I have no comment. Why don't you find out? You have all the resources, don't you?

It was an impressive and bravura performance – at times taciturn, at times hysterical – always pleading innocence. Chapman too played a fine supporting role: calm, efficient, unperturbed by the histrionics played out in front of him.

The SIO had one last line of enquiry to pursue, one last strand of Rotardier's web to unpick before he could take the case to the jury.

He ordered checks on every Fairfax Road – the street Rotardier claimed Hamilton to be living in since his return from France. There turned out to be four in London. Each house in each street was visited: there was no trace of David Hamilton and never had been.

On Thursday, 28 January 1988, a jury at the Central London Criminal Court – the Old Bailey – convicted Kingsley Ignatius Rotardier of the murder of David Napier Hamilton. The presiding judge, Sir James Miskin, Recorder of London, imposed the mandatory sentence of life imprisonment and added a recommendation that the killer serve a minimum of twenty years.

Kingsley Ignatius Rotardier had a one-word comment when asked if he had anything to say: 'Pillocks,' he spat at the jury, before two prison officers led him away.

Chief Superintendent Robert Chapman leans back in his chair at Croydon Golf Club and lights another Rothman's. Promoted since his success in the Hamilton case, he now heads the AMIP which he joined just as it began.

The Rotardier case is one he enjoys telling: it is a case in a million, a true detective story for true detectives. No need for fancy forensic science or clever psychological profile: just 'good coppering' of the sort that every policeman believes they are capable.

'There is,' he opines, 'no such thing as the perfect murder. Killers are by and large amateurs. It is the detectives who are the professionals. It is we who understand the business of murder.'

8
The Future
of Murder

There is no simple description of the
people who are convicted of murder, or of
their victims or the surrounding
circumstances. It would be very convenient
if we could identify simple categories of
murder and murderers, but only a
superficial type of classification seems
possible . . . There is not a simple stereotypical
murderer.

*Dr Barry Mitchell, senior lecturer in law at
Coventry Polytechnic*

Why murder? What is it about the five cases we have
presented here which so persuaded us of their importance as to
devote a chapter to each? Why in any event, write about so
disturbing a crime?

The answer is simply that we have much to learn, of murder
in general and from these cases in particular. It has been a
constant source of surprise to us, as we waded through file after
file, report after report, that so little formal and academic
research has been carried out into murder in Britain.

As Dr Barry Mitchell, author of the most recent limited
study† of how men murder and what happens to them
thereafter, discovered:

† *Murder and Penal Policy*, Macmillan, London 1990.

There has been virtually no reliable assessment of the issue of murder. Despite all the fictional writing on the subject, the academic community has paid little attention to it.

My study, perhaps not surprisingly, showed that murder was an extremely diverse crime, not merely in its obvious characteristics – who actually kills whom – but in the gravity of cases that it encompasses.

There is no simple description of the people who are convicted of murder, or of their victims or the surrounding circumstances. It would be very convenient if we could identify simple categories of murder and murderers, but only a superficial type of classification seems possible.

I discovered that it was relatively uncommon for there to be any statistical significance in the correlation between even two factors in a series of individual cases. Admittedly there were a number of cases which seemed to have the same characteristics – for example, there were several murders committed by young men, many of whom were unemployed, who apparently killed for financial gain. Many of their victims were late-middle-aged or even elderly people, killed in their own homes.

But many other young male murderers committed very different types of homicide offences, and many of them had a job; equally many victims aged 50 or more were killed by older offenders, and for seemingly different reasons at that. There is not a simple stereotypical murderer.

With one caveat we would accept and support Dr Mitchell's analysis. For the vast and overwhelming majority of unlawful killings there is one common factor: murder is most usually carried out by men; women murderers are rare in the extreme – generally fewer than 10 per cent in any given year.

This macho, laddish element to the act of unlawful killing is reflected in the subsequent investigation and prosecution of cases. Women murder squad detectives – at least at senior ranks – are a rare species nationally. In London, at present, they are almost non-existent. Women judges, too, are few and far between. And women politicians, framing the laws which the police and courts must enforce, are a tiny minority of those who sit in parliament.

The result is a certain 'boysie' feel to the entire process. Lads kill people, and lads investigate killings; elderly men sit in

judgement wrapped in ceremonially male clothing and per-
petuate injustice like that endured by Sara Thornton and
others with her.

The aim of this chapter is to analyse what more we can do to
make the business of murder – that is to say its prevention,
detection and prosecution – more efficient.

We need from the outset to recognise that it is already highly
efficient in terms of clear-up rates. More than 93 per cent of
cases of murder are reported 'cleared-up' by police forces
throughout England and Wales annually.

But not only are there other cases – cases which should be
called murder, cases which remain unsolved – but the proces-
ses involved in this business of detection can be clumsy and
drawn-out.

The purpose of each case in this book has been to highlight an
existing problem within the systems of murder investigation.
But before we come to those specifics, we should perhaps re-
examine the very concept of murder itself.

We saw at the beginning of this book that murder is not a
written statute law, but merely the opinion of a sixteenth-
century legal journalist. In turn this has led to confusion and
inefficiency, and the inability to draw a reliable line between it
and manslaughter. It seems clear that the law is overdue for an
extensive overhaul. Nor is it difficult to see how to reform the
present chaotic and inequitable lottery.

The United States has a system of varying degrees of
murder. The idea of this series of levels is to introduce the
notion of an increasingly serious offence – murder one being
more serious than, say, murder three.

The cutting edge of the system is in the ill-understood
concept of premeditation. English law is based on the idea of
'malice aforethought' – even though there need be neither
malice nor aforethought as either word is understood in
common parlance.

It would take only a simple redefinition – ideally within a
new statutory offence of murder – for this to be made relevant
and comprehensible: homicide should only become murder

where there is a provable prior willingness to kill. We need to realise that this redefinition might exclude cases like that of Brett White. The remainder would fall into the catch-all of manslaughter.

The conventional argument against this has been that the British public believes murder should remain a heinous and severely punished offence. But no empirical survey has yet been taken of the British public's view on murder policy – though if it were to be, all available anecdotal evidence suggests the overwhelming majority would vote for the return of capital punishment. But even this difficulty is not insoluble. The present distinction between murder and manslaughter – in practice if not in theory – is in the sentence, not the motive. Whatever the neat and tidy arguments over *mens rea* and malice aforethought, it is the difference between a mandatory life sentence and a sliding scale of probation, fines and prison which truly sets the two apart.

Most western nations retain – where the death penalty has been abolished – the life sentence for murder. But in many this sentence is a maximum, an option available to the trial judge rather than a mandatory imposition from which there is no escape.

The Australian state of New South Wales has shown in a working experiment that providing this flexibility to courts has had beneficial rather than detrimental effects. It is time we took the same route.

For these large reforms to be adopted does, of course, depend on the Home Office.

It was hard, in the months we spent with police officers researching individual cases, to find working detectives with any real respect for the department which, in theory, guides policing. Changing the course of Home Office policy is akin to attempting a three-point turn in an oil tanker – technically feasible, but practically impossible. And yet change is needed. One of the very first lessons from the case histories we have recounted is the need for a greater awareness of the problem of sexual offending.

John Dunne, the killer of Lorraine Benson, is clearly a dangerous man. His pattern of previous offending points to an escalating aberrant urge: such urges are not controlled without effort, and certainly cannot be simply 'punished away'.

In his letters to us Dunne himself has recognised the potential benefits of good psycho-sexual counselling. But it is far from certain whether he will get it. The Home Office claims that there are four psychologists in Albany Prison ready to work with him should he make such a request. It will not, however, say whether he is receiving any counselling. The likelihood is that he is not. It is a long step from accepting the advisability of treatment to actually starting the process. Sexual offenders do not tend – unprompted – to seek out the process which would control their cycles of behaviour. Yet unless such work is undertaken, John Dunne is almost certain to kill again if the right circumstances arise.

We would argue that, whilst it is not practicable to force sex offenders into mandatory therapy, there ought to be an element of *de facto* compulsion – a 'Hobson's Choice' which encourages them to choose counselling in favour of a less comfortable option, perhaps a regime which is more physically severe than that which exists in sexual therapy treatment units.

In return for this sort of dynamism from the prison department of the Home Office, the public must also begin to understand the reality of sexual offending. It is no longer simply enough to complain when a man abuses a woman or a child and subsequently to denounce the very notion of spending money on his therapy. We must move away from the idea that the provision of psycho-sexual counselling to offenders somehow implies sympathy with them or their actions: it does not. Instead it reflects a fear of there being further victims in the future if nothing is done now.

Such wider understanding cannot come about in the present system of sealing off offenders from the world outside. When we queried the Home Office's refusal to allow an interview with John Dunne – an interview which he had already agreed to

– officials quoted Prison Service Standing Order No. 5:

> Visits to inmates by journalists or authors in their
> professional capacity should in general not be allowed . . . if a
> journalist or author who is a friend or relative wishes to visit
> an inmate in this capacity and not for professional purposes,
> the governor should inform the intending visitor that before
> the visit can take place he or she will be required to give a
> written undertaking that any material obtained at the
> interview will not be used for professional purposes and in
> particular for publication by the intending visitor or anyone
> else.

That this rule has no statutory force – it is simply a regulation
made up by the Home Office for its own convenience, and is
selectively applied – is typical of the blinkered lack of thought
which surrounds the issue of offenders. Locking men away for
up to twenty years is no guarantee of removing the twisted
desire which may have led them there in the first place.
Denying the public information about them is a certain way of
ensuring that ignorance and misunderstanding prevent the
universal deployment of successful therapy programmes.

The second overall lesson we learned from our research is that
by and large policemen tend not to ask the larger question
'why?'. Murder investigation concerns, it would seem, questions of who, how, where and with what? – but rarely enquires
into the motivation behind the offence. On those rare occasions
when this happens, it is all too often seen as a mere technique
to nullify potential defence arguments.

Yet we have seen, in cases like that of Michele Lupo, that
even in the most bizarre of serial murderers there lurks a
motivation. It may not be rational, it may not be pleasant, but
for the act of killing another human being there is always a
reason. Find the reason, study it and understand it, and the
possibility exists of preventing similar offences or tracking
down other killers with a matching mental process.

The FBI set up its Behavioral Science Academy in Virginia
to do just that. In Britain – though most regional forces have
training colleges hosting *ad hoc* lectures and short courses –

there is little or no in-house criminological research or analysis. The same is true of psyschoanalytic studies and profiling.

The single, simple way to stop this gap is to set up what Trenchard envisaged nearly sixty years ago: a national police training college working full-time on research and development of the scientific advances in the field of psychological motivation.

If the mysterious skills of the forensic scientist can be accepted within the police force, then there is no reason to reject their psychological counterparts.

It follows – logically – from the above, that a national police force in some shape or form is likely to emerge. Whilst we would support the need for some national policing – most notably in the fields of paedophilia and child abuse – neither we as authors, nor the AMIP teams as professional detectives can see the need to set up national murder squads akin to some of those established within the FBI. Every case we have researched involved some basis of local knowledge: a national response would be likely to overlook this local need.

That said, there is a case for a long hard look being taken at the policing of murder throughout Britain. AMIPs have proved extremely successful in the five years they have operated within London. Other major cities could undoubtedly benefit from the immense and dedicated strength such squads bring to a homicide investigation.

However, not all in the AMIP system is rosy. Individual chief superintendents – one, remember, for each of the eight areas within the Metropolitan Police – have no power or control over the deployment of detectives in the divisions on which they are based. Yet it is precisely on these divisional officers that the AMIPs rely when a new investigation begins.

And internal rivalry still dogs the Force. Bob Chapman, with barely a pause for thought, is able to recount several occasions when sheer bloody-mindedness on the part of 'rival' areas has severely hampered his effectiveness. In one such case the refusal of enough officers to mount a surveillance on the house of a suspected killer led to him escaping the net and attempting another murder.

Such rivalries are, in themselves, signs of the macho culture that dominates the police force. There is no easy solution to this problem – but problem it is. Simply promoting more women into positions of authority will not overnight remove the laddish distrust – more probably a deep-seated male insecurity – with which many experienced officers view women police. Nor, in murder squads at least, will it provide an answer to the logistical difficulties many women face in bringing up children whilst at the same time performing a job which obstinately refuses to obey office hours.

The old male culture which prevented adequate police response to incidents of abuse of women – cases like that of Jini Cooppen – may now be dying out. Certainly, the Metropolitan Police is in the vanguard of positive responses based on the automatic arrest of a violent man in or outside the home.

Yet, again, this long overdue realism is not being matched by the Home Office, which will not fund enough women's shelters to provide adequate sanctuary for the victims of male violence. Most shelters now exist on stretched budgets provided by local authorities, charities and private donation. The attitude of the Home Office is all the less comprehensible given that it does recognise that domestic violence is part of a vicious cycle of abuse whose end is quite frequently murder.

And it is this argument of interconnection which is at the heart of the lessons we should draw from the work of murder squads like that in Croydon. The act of killing is rarely an isolated event: it does not occur in a vacuum. It is part of a larger process-shaping the offender's perceptions and behaviour.

Whilst in some areas it may be impractical to think in terms of researching policies which seek to defuse the recognisable and predictable patterns which may lead to murder, in just as many others it makes moral, political and even financial sense.

If more had been known about the nature of sadistic homosexual killers, might Michele Lupo have been caught before he killed so many young men?

If longer-term shelter – or at the least good advice – had been available to Jini Cooppen, might she be alive today?

If thorough psycho-sexual counselling had been provided to John Dunne in Glenthorne, might he have learnt to control his offending, and Lorraine Benson be with her family and friends still?

If goverments – of whatever political persuasion – could only grasp that their policies, financial and social, have a formative effect on the population in whose name they rule, might Brett White have grown up differently, and Noel Christopher not have died?

Hypothetical questions, but questions which are repeated daily as each new homicide is reported and investigated. This year there will be an average of more than ten unlawful killings a week – almost two every day.

The cost of the investigations alone is incalculable: Bob Chapman has no reliable estimate of how much the enquiry into the disappearance and presumed death of David Hamilton cost the taxpayer.

But the cost of doing nothing is far higher still. Policing – be it by AMIP, Division or by local beat bobbies – is part of the answer. Providing information, understanding and research, the other vital ingredient. There is no one solution: but until all government and law enforcement agencies work out the question together there is little prospect of reducing the ever rising rate of violent death.

Index